MW00526879

Out of the Shadows

from darkness to light

Leon Gregori

OUT OF THE SHADOWS: FROM DARKNESS TO LIGHT

© Leon Gregori 2019. All rights reserved.

The right of Leon Gregori to be identified as the author of this work
has been asserted by him in accordance with the Copyright,
Designs and Patents Act 1988.

First Published in 2019 by the Soulful Group
"we unlace words & detangle life"

www.soulfulgroup.com

Cover illustration by Raktim Parashar

ISBN-13: 978-1-9998104-8-1

—

DEDICATION

To Jennifer Jones, for taking me from darkness to light.

MESSAGE FROM THE AUTHOR

I have been writing since my mid-teens and I have always found it completely natural to express myself through creative writing (as opposed to keeping a factual diary). However, I was always very hesitant and shy regarding my work and prior to the start of this publication process, only a select few family and friends had seen any of my poems.

My poetry has always been unpredictable and without structure. I suppose you could call it *freestyle prose* although many of my poems have *rhythmic tendencies*. Every poem originates entirely from the random moments in my life when I have felt compelled to write hence the poems differ in length. I have never set aside time to write but I have always kept my notepad nearby to capture these random moments as they entered my mind.

My poems predominately cover the theme of *love and heartbreak* and the *healing* that needs to come with such intense emotions. The poems feature in this book largely in chronological order and I have selected to present them across seven chapters as these represent seven distinct shifts in my life thus far.

After a lifetime in the shadows I feel like now is the time to share my work, with the hope of inspiring and ultimately helping others who have experienced the same.

ACKNOWLEDGMENTS

I thank Ria Worley for encouraging me to attend the first book launch hosted by the Soulful Group and Katie White for inspiring the cover artwork; both have greatly supported me on this exciting new journey.

I thank the incredibly talented Raktim Parashar for the cover illustration and the Soulful Group for taking me on as one of their foundational authors; they brought my vision to life and have turned this publishing dream into a reality.

I thank those who have showered me with warmth and love over the years. Those who have inspired me, even when they did not know they were doing so. Those I feel humbled to hold in my memory. I thank those I have trusted, those I have cherished and those who have touched my soul.

I thank 'love' for it has shown me life for how it should be seen. I am so proud and honored to have loved because without experiencing it, my work and this book would never have evolved.

I thank my Mother and family for bringing me into this world and for raising me. For giving me life and teaching me how to live it. For showing me love, support and for giving me the platform to succeed.

CONTENTS

Follow My Writing Journey

Instagram @leon.gregori213
Facebook @leon.gregori213
www.allpoetry.com/Leon_Gregori

CHAPTER ONE

THE BEGINNING

My first poem emerged without warning when I was just fifteen years old. I still recall the moment 'the voice' came into my mind and I was instantly compelled to write. I would regularly wake up to scraps of paper or an open laptop with no idea how the words managed to turn from voices in my mind to poems onto pages. Back then, I didn't think too deeply about the process; I just went with the flow. All I knew for sure is that these words were a precious secret that I needed to hide and protect. I felt the words were too 'grown-up' to share with others; my thoughts and feelings as an adolescent, predominantly centred around love and my search for it. I convinced myself that only love could heal my damaged soul; a soul that was bruised by an unforgiving world. But my lack of self-confidence was chronic, and I was often confused, lonely and lost whilst searching for the purpose I doubted I would ever be worthy of.

These seven poems express my journey of *self-discovery*:

1. DISTORTED
2. MY SOUL
3. ANGELS
4. MOTHER
5. FAITH
6. IDEOLOGY
7. OUR RACE IS NOT ONE

DISTORTED

My mind, full of thoughts
Crazy theories
Intent and instinct
It controls my body, determines my life
Holds all of my issues and prominence
Incorporates my pride and enforces my ideas
It helps communicate, distinguish and recreate
It tells me what I like and what I do not
What I want and what I do not
It forms my values and my traditions
My instructions and detail
My mind controls me
It controls my existence
It controls my life

But to all of an entity
There must be bad
To all of good
To all of sense
And to all of man
There must be bad
And to my mind
There is bad

But for me it is memories
To me it is me
An outcast
Different and strange
Weird and wrong
Or distorted
In one

As my mind forms my body
My appearance and my expression
My image and my impressions
It forms not of my heart
My feeling and emotion
No, it does not
Form the core of my soul

For me I have two entities
My mind
And the core of my soul
And both are unified
Powerful and glorious
Together and united
Together
Though distorted
In one

MY SOUL

And so I feel
Through my mind travels my soul
My soul of heart and emotion
And through my mind spurs action
Driven by the effervescence of my sentiment

And I am here
And now my feeling is driving through the vision of one true article
One true image
And of all I feel is that for the goddess
The female
The nation
The world of which we offer
To the fingertips of their generation
Their generation of beauty
Magnificence
Splendor
Grandeur
Our creators and our lives

I do not feel myself
I feel a power
A power of help
To help our architects
From the vile of their own children
From their own blood
Pieces from their heart
Their offspring and their genes

Man, men
Male
Me

And it hurts

We hurt

ANGELS

Our world explodes with beauty
Nature is nice
In the scenes of sun
Warmth and glory
We admire and grasp
Picture and hold
We write of the strength
And of the artefact

We write of the scene
That fills us with a glow
A ray of light
A sensation of ecstasy
Enticing our hearts
And plucking our veins
Infiltrating our lungs
And seeping through its walls
Joining our blood
And creeping towards our heart
Our system tingles
It spreads through our body
From head to toe
It is there
A sensation
Delight
And joy

It purses our lips
Massages our muscles
A gentle touch
Smooth
And delicate

And you wonder now
Of what sensation
Of what scene
Please read with intent

18

Because you see every day
You see of the scene
Of the voice
Of the light and ecstasy
And as you feel a smile
Encourage your mind
Let instinct entourage
Let it be your guide
Open your eyes
For you will see
A woman in her stride
As beautiful as can be

MOTHER

A woman in her stride
Here we see
In this small part
All evil will flee

All fate and hurt
Repent and sorrow
All fear and power
Straight and narrow

I feel for our mothers
In my deepest sensation
I hear their cries
Calls of desperation

Calls for respect
Kindness and understanding
To be nurtured and protected
Comforted and enchanted

For they are our mothers
For them we breathe
For them we connect
It is them that lead

And for our creators
Our sparkle
Our gust and our guile
The spring in our step
And the long-lasting mile

The mile of life
So they are
Our only future
The one true star

The element of life
They form us as one
With no distinction or reaction
They will never run

Here from the beginning
They envisaged life as a dream
To stand tall in far future
To advance as a team

They hold our existence
Form nature and true beauty
Without them our being
Would hold almost no continuity

We would not survive
Or flourish and stand tall
We would not strive and engineer a future
We would not move forward at all

For they have ensured our future as one
They have added the light, the glamour and fun
They have entailed charm and splendor
All we have created is war and the dollar

They gave birth to man
And thy must follow its mother
Hold glory and respect
Cherish and honor

Respect and protect
Bear love and trust
Hold a gentle hand in faith
Unanimity is a must

But for them trust our lives
Our souls and our minds
For our beautiful women
Have created this very moment in time

FAITH

Religion is a powerful vision
It holds the hearts and souls of those who see it true
It controls their spirits and views of life
They know not different
And their trust bears God and him holy

But to contest such a view
Its control and manner
A man-made feast
And political correctness
Is such a product of government
Human power and greed
In our minds such elements will always run free
Written and published
Sold and exploited
Such a way grips life and we know not different
For years to come our children are forced into such dire belief
Surrounded by preachers and the gold of Gods house

I challenge this entity
A man-made thought
I believe in love and life as our own
Our minds are our Gods
We control our own destiny
We will strive and we will create
As a human race our universe should be explored
We should not fall victim to pure fantasy
But fall behind to advancement for humanity

Jesus was a savior
He gave belief to millions who believed in life as hopeless
He restored visions to those disillusioned
But continued belief has waned too long; we have become restless
Waiting for the day when our minds break free
Soon we will follow and reject this conspiracy
Conflict and blasphemy will no longer control this hapless world
One day we will realize what is scientifically real

We are only humans
Tried and tested
And our only self-invasion
Is through our own minds and souls

We create future
And our own destiny
We live not in a book of ancient history
Man-made words must not be heeded
Believe in ourselves and the day will come
A day of God, our minds will be needed

When I think of life there is so much to question
So much to bear
And so much decision
I think of its points
Its trust and necessity
And I believe there is none
But true love and entity

IDEOLOGY

In time I will find
An aim to my life
In time it will ensue
An image will entice

My mind is what holds me
My mind which holds fair
An image of life
Too much to bear

This rancid society
True to most
I believe is not right
An image of a ghost

This society of ours
Holds no value
It holds no morals
Or words of virtue

Thus, it holds
Just a simple light
Birth of money
Discrimination and fight

This is not life that we hold
It is simple squalor
For those who long to greed
And those who should know better

A victim to those
Trapped in this world
They know not different
But a dream of diamonds and pearls

These are not values
This is not life
It is a core of materials
Which dominate in sight

It is that which I question
That which I do not uphold
I question your life
All you've ever known

For me life is such
Of future and love
It differs from most
From your mind and your ghost

I want to shine
For love in its own
For me at this time
It's that of which shows

The basis of life
Is to acknowledge as men
That women are our life
Our struggle to comprehend

We must understand that without the meaning
We cannot live life, or the world it is dreaming
We cannot chase gold, jewels or riches
We can only trust ourselves, women and creatures

Let's strive for advance
Creation and ideology
Let's not be trapped, enticed domestically
Let's strive for advance, venture universally

Let's look to our world
Our adaptation and existence
Relay the past
Pity those distant

Let's come together
And feel a new life
We need to uphold
Love in its right

We need to uphold
Our mind as our God
It is that which strengthens
But a trust we've now lost

Our mind is what we have
Along with our souls
And then there are each other
To joy but not fold

We cannot forget
True love and entity
We must not fall
It is with us all

I wish it true
Love as an entity
The only tragedy
Is that we believe it not necessity

OUR RACE IS NOT ONE

Am I doomed for loneliness
Doomed for no star
Is this world in its oyster
Flawed in deep tar
For I feel no love
I feel no life

But instead there is pain
And suffering rife
There is a world
This grips us all
It abandons love
It rises to call
It leads us in pain
But it fails to guide
It disguises our tails
That strive to collide

It grips and holds
But toils and brawls
But where is this world that that grips us all
I wish to guide
As I wish to seek
A new world of living
A world in its peace
I pray for the day
I pray for the night
When we all start to realize
Our minds hold the might
Are minds as I've quoted
True mysteries
We hold many thoughts
And indecencies

But in those minds
Peace should prevail
We should all come to the conclusion
That we should not fail

But we should walk forward
As one human race
Abolish such squalors
Come together in wake
Deny this insipid fighting
Money and war
Cherish our lives
Bring love to our doors

I believe we should move forward
Together as one
One as a race
Discrimination undone
But what should we do with such precious entity
Throw it aside
And strive for unanimity

But yes, that is of truth
That is our destiny
Collaborate as one
Journey in whole
Explore our boundaries
Drive till we fold
We must explore our world
Our universe and souls
Ignore our fantasy boundaries
Money is old
Indifference is old
As is all trade
It is a free world
Just peace is our gain

As a race we should not starve
And we should not fall
But we should feel that of nature
We should feel it all
We should feel
This world in its oyster
For what it ferments
Our lives are a canter

Our lives are gifted
With talent and luxury
Knowledge and love
Not trade and industry
Let's not waste our time
Creating a fantasy
Let's come together
And rule out this apathy

Come together
All resources as one
Explore our universe
Reach out to the sun
In intelligence we altercate
For our universe reveals nothing
Darkness and stars, curiosity and fate
Emotion and loving, life and its plate

Our universe is large
It is not small
Glorified space
Brightness and awe
It has no boundaries
It has no walls
But we must remember
It covers us all

We have no control
We have no leaders
The universe and life
Will eventually free us
Exploration and intelligence
New life and new science
Squander in squalor

Our race is not one
There is but more life
In this galaxy of stars
Collaborate our darkness
And break it for it is farce
Our intelligence is dire
But soon will prevail
As our future will enclose
New life will entail

CHAPTER TWO

CHASING LOVE

I was now 17 and had just left school. I longed for independence and wanted to start my career and build my life. This drove me, but ultimately it was the concept of love that was like a never-ending blissful dream which empowered me every morning. In many ways, up until this point, my life had been a 'world of chaos' but I was growing-up fast and when I thought of my purpose, there was always a ray of sunshine to be found. I now knew the childhood battle I experienced had been preparing me for this. All else was incidental and my sole purpose was to love someone and to be loved back. It really was that simple. But how would I find love in my less than ordinary life? Only confident, young men found love, not those who struggled with self-belief each day. Oscillating between feeling 'destined for love' and simultaneously feeling it was 'out of my reach' was exhausting. A heady cocktail of elation, excitement, nerves and fear simultaneously attacked my consciousness. I was blissfully unaware of my surroundings and became embroiled on a long and painful path to becoming the man I always wanted to be. Yet it was here, in my most turbulent years, that my expression of love was at its purest.

These nine poems express my journey of *pursuit*:

1. MY FUTURE
2. A DECLARATION OF LOVE
3. FOR LOVE I MAY FIND
4. THE FANTASY OF LOVE
5. A SILVER LINING
6. EMOTIONS IN MOTION
7. CLOSE MY EYES
8. MY MASK
9. A WORLD OF AN ANGEL

MY FUTURE

And so, for my future
Gone is my birth
My thoughts
And feelings so true
Adamant is my future
Only of love
For I feel no other life
No other joy
No other passion or no other destiny
My future is my love

My love I search for
Love I so wish to find
To make my heart complete
And inspire my soul
To find a star
To share it and contain it
For my love has the power
And the power has me

And that is my future
Love in its way
A stunning emotion
A stunning word
So much is its influence, power and awe
And that is my life
Future and all

A DECLARATION OF LOVE

Where do I begin, where do I start
Every time I look at you
Hear your name or listen to your voice
I get these mad thoughts
Crazy feelings bubbling inside me
Whatever I am doing
Or wherever I am going
Any path I take, I see only you by my side

Everything about you is so special
You may find it hard to believe
But if you can find it in your heart to trust me
It would not be so hard to see

It is tearing me up inside
Knowing you do not feel the same
Every day I wake up and tell myself
That maybe your feelings have changed
It has yet to happen
But the clock is still ticking
Surely there can be a chance
A dawn, a new beginning

How I can be complaining
When surely, I have enough
I have an amazing friend in you
I am so proud to know such a queen
Honored when we speak
When I see your stunning face
I look into your eyes and wonder
How anyone could ever mistreat you
Such a wonderful being
Breathtaking in every way

A woman like you does not come around often
In this ever-changing life
And when there comes a chance of happiness
Surely, I should grab it with both hands
I must take the chance
Even though it is a gamble
Or shall I miss it and repent
Spend a lifetime of regret

Would it change our relationship
If I was to be honest about how I feel
If my heart was a book shall I read it
Spend hours on what it reveals

Let me be open and let me expose
Let me speak feelings so true
Cupid has spoken and my soul has responded
Angel I am falling for you

FOR LOVE I MAY FIND

Your love for wanting and your love for wake
I cherish the moments and the steps you take
You are special and you are my entity
More than a friend, your love is a specialty

Your words are diamonds raining from the sky
Words to ponder and words to cry
The peace you give and the thoughts you express
Show but to all of nature that you grace and impress

A nature of kindness and a nature of warmth
An infinite wisdom and a direction of north
A direction of north, for we will forever move forward
We now have a path, one which no one can break

Our friendship is unique, you mean so much
Your word, your soul and your touch
For you touch me in mind and you touch me in soul
For all the want in the world you've given me a heart of gold

Stunning sweet rose, you have such an honorable name
You've acquired my wanting and given me fame
Just to know you is such an honor
You're someone I've longed for, a person of splendor

How I've cried and how I have missed
The emptiness I have felt has disclosed my bliss
I've had a hard life and I've felt infinite pain
But for you my future would have little gain

But here you are
You inspire my thoughts
My emotions and values
My discontent is now naught

You are the entity I have always craved
I've missed such company; I've lived such a maze
Every thought I now have, and my impressions of the world
Now include you, for you're my sparkling pearl

You are the highest angel
Your light spreads rife
And all I can say
Is stay sweet for life

THE FANTASY OF LOVE

May I collaborate and remember
Your one true fantasy
Your dream of love
And symbol of ecstasy

May I present your dream
And allow your vision
To express itself in words
And believe its mission

For you have a want
To aid your smile
For you have a want
To relive such guile

There is a dream
Of meeting true love
A dream to announce
To your mind above

To announce such emotion
Belief and strength
That your search is over
And your hurt can repent

Feelings then form
To build on your dream
Between you and your love
A journey it seems

A place of comfort
And a place of longing
To be alone at last
Only privacy is joining

As you move up close
Together at last
You join in strength
Your souls join fast

You sit underneath
The protection of life
Look up to the sky
Feel warmth and entice

An entice to the stars
Love and effigy
Your time at last
Love streams from your energy

Your heart feels its time
You feel each other's heartbeat
Your heat and excitement
Soothing a treat

The gentle lap of beach waves
In a timely distance
And the lap of two hearts
The only in existence

A SILVER LINING

I do not want to wait
Patience has never been a virtue
A second must not be wasted
The test of true love can be cruel
My dream is to hold you tight
And never let you go

I feel you constantly
Your scent I smell and breathe
I close my eyes and see you
Open them and imagine you
You are a permanent vision
The light that reveals my heart

You are the voice that calms me
The candle that warms my soul
It is so soothing
That thought that is constantly thought
The desire within my mind
That never goes away
I just miss your very essence
Your heart, your mind, your soul

The atmosphere that surrounds you
Just so powerful and strong
So calm and precious
Perfect in every way
Our hearts beat as one
So together we must be
A force of life we are
Stand the test of time we will

Always on our cloud
Forever promoting our silver lining
Our atmosphere is one that knows nothing but to shine
There is a candle inside my soul
That was lit by you
The candle is still burning
Still standing tall

EMOTIONS IN MOTION

Life...I never know
I never understand
Without my heart I am losing myself
Without my angel, I am dying
I cannot be here
Where she is, so is life

She is fragments of perfection, a fantasy of amazement and solitude
This place has such a stunning strain, such a pressure
That pressure is happiness
A pressure of finding maintenance
And consistency, in the emotion of love

When I motivate myself to a level
Whereby I can cope with the influence of the outside world
My shoulders crumble to gravity
This burden hurts
People die
People cry
People are hurt
The emotion hurts
Without her I must succumb to this world
A world of which is nothing...nothing...without her
I love her but I find her love so hard to trust

I've felt so many tears
I find it hard to accept that someone actually loves me for who I am
Such a powerful emotion
Love is perhaps the height of our creation
Us as humans, to feel such a bond towards a separate body
A separate soul
A separate entity
It is supernatural
To feel so heightened
Ecstatic

———

Truly beyond boundaries at just the thought
Just the sight
How beautiful can one be
How powerful, how definitive
What a splendid being
What a creation
A true goddess
With her life spurns my true love
So wonderful
So beautiful

CLOSE MY EYES

Close my eyes
Sweet goodnight
Is it a dream
Of an angel so bright
As I lay on my bed
I wonder why
What have I done
To reach the sky
For I have done just that
In meeting you
Soared to the heavens
To a height so new
This new life you bring
These tears of joy
This wonderful smile
This love we employ
And as I lay here
I always remember
The dark side of life
Raw nerves so tender
So painful the sights
So hurtful were those scenes
They used to haunt me
Purge my dreams
But you came along
To sweep me from earth
You came along
I joined your berth
Your warm sweet smile
Your wondrous nature
This true prowess
So amazing your gender
At first, I thought
As a woman you were natural
Always stunning
Your essence so factual
Factual of a woman
So full of entice

Typical in emotion
So natural, so nice
But then I thought
My heart started to question
Was this the start
Life earning redemption
Had fate decided
For a beautiful twist
My soul to find equal
Never ending bliss
Was I about
To see my dream
My true love
One sparkling stream
A stream of awe
You soon became
My knees went weak
As I repeated your name
My body trembled
My heart started pounding
Love at first sight
Simply astounding
Our adventure began
On a warm summer night
We joined in forces
A light so bright
We took the world by storm
And never looked back
Through thick and thin
We always stay on track
Our smiles are so strong
Our unity unbreakable
Such a pure bond
Love irreplaceable
We laugh and we gage
In this pure fantasy
We tremble when passion
Reaches pure ecstasy
Your touch soothes my mind
Full of dangerous thoughts

You banish them far
Never to be caught
No more hurt
No more pain
No more hate
No more rain
Is this a dream
Or is it real
Do I care
For I still feel
I can feel this motion
This strength and energy
You are the one
A stunning effigy
Whether my eyes awaken
Or my body shuts down
I will always feel taken
By an angel in town
An angel so awesome
Love so sweet
Always in life
I bow to her feet
My body and mind
My heart and my soul
Dedicated to her
And her story untold
A story of how
To reach such glory
Of how to maintain
A perfect furore
Because as she awakens
And her beauty roars
Diamonds sparkle
Nature applauds
How can earth
House such a queen
We are so humble
Scared to be seen
How can we grace
Her perfect presence

How can I embrace
Her wondrous essence
I ponder this prospect
Of warming her heart
I await her perception
Of us never being apart
She says she loves me
And I love her back
Have I won
Are we still intact
I wake up now
And revise my life
I am in love
No more strife
Yes I see
It must be true
Yes I am
I am in love with you
I tell myself this
All of these pages
Just to realize
As I crawl through the stages
These stages of life
These hours these minutes
I have to remind
Of us and our stitches
Our stitches of life
And our grains of love
Every second I recite
This poem above
Am I still dreaming
Or truly awake
I must understand now
My heart is at stake
Sleep starts to beckon
I am beginning to tire
I want a good dream
Of love so near
A dream of perfection
Of every detail of life

Every second of happiness
A hug so tight
I want to smile
Whilst every other muscle relaxes
I want to feel protected
Warm and fantastic
How can I do this
How can I dream
Of this perception
This true love stream
There must be a way
To dominate with ease
There must be a way
To conquer with peace
To feel the sigh
The breath of an angel
To feel the fire
The strength of her mantle
I must believe
In her heart
Believe in her want
For us never to part
I must whisper sweet words
Language from god
Pray and remember
How chance came and got
Got our two hearts
And merged them as one
Gave me a formula
To dream with the sun
I must spell her name
That I do
Envisage her spirit
That is the cue
My heart begins to pound
Oh yes, it is true
Oh, how I will sleep sweet and sound
Forever loving you

MY MASK

Do you see my mask
Covered in pain
Do you see the hurt
The constant rain
The dark black clouds
Circled me endlessly
I had no choice
It drained my energy
But for my soulmate
I would have given up
Finished the ritual
Deepened the cut
There is so much more
To be written and explained
A longer tale
But no pleasure gained

No matter what I write
Or what I portray
Nothing can bring to light
The truth of this present day
I cannot present
My undying love
Love cannot be explained
Written or trained
It can only be expressed
And judged by the world
Actions speak louder
Than words could ever tell
Off with the mask
Sweet angel I love you
Now and forever
God it is so true

A WORLD OF AN ANGEL

This world of wonder
That lies in your wake
This world of wisdom
Awaiting your grace
This world and its core
Confronts your being
Beckons your soul
Feeling is believing
I feel it at heart
I feel it so bold
I feel it in wisdom
I feel it in soul
And then I feel you
Your word
Your essence
Your aura is true
You bring a mind to me
You've revived my soul
Brought joy to my mind
Peace to my fold
My heart bears a beat
For every breath you take
It calls a duty
To this world at your wake
As I embark on a journey
Of life in this world
My source reads a heart
Its goal reads a girl
Your heart I await
Your goal I uphold
For I wish I was with you
To ferment my soul
You bring me such joy
You've ended my pain
A life of no love
Precious small gain

I wish you would never
Ever feel such pain
I hope to protect
And always bring you gain
And as we met
In simple words
Hello beautiful
Spurns every verse
Hello beautiful
Do I live your dream
For my dream is not mine
It's ours it seems
This world of wonder
That adheres to your wake
Has brought us together
I wish it not fate
I wish it not fate
But simple entity
Written into our lives
With endless energy
A time of glory
Your life stuns all
Not least that of mine
I await your beck and call
Your heart warms mine
Your heart warms all
Your life to cherish
Your life and your soul

CHAPTER THREE

BROKEN

I had just entered my twenties. The world around me was still in chaos, yet my career was rising, giving me the tools to carve my own path. It was here that life had become truly beautiful; I was not just 'in love', I was consumed by it. My world had become smaller and safer than ever before. Each morning I danced on 'cloud-nine' and each night I bowed to my 'heaven on earth'. But as I embraced this new existence, I always knew deep down that my love was not immune to turbulence. It was like an air of reality that only I could sense. Indeed, I was permitted happiness only for a fleeting moment. The love I eagerly chased for so many years was crashing and burning. All that was left was a hollow shell where my beating heart once lived. I was devastated and with it my writing took a dark turn. My joyous emotions were replaced with hate. I tried with logic to wish it away, but my soul did not allow it. I just had to experience it. I had to befriend the demons to understand them. Only if I understood them could I understand myself, so I allowed the walls of my heart to cave in. With the collapse they opened boxes in my mind that I had long left buried.

These ten poems express my journey into *heartbreak*:

1. IF HE CALLS HER
2. BROKEN HEART
3. HAPPINESS
4. HEARTBREAKER
5. INSANE
6. THE BIRDS FROM OUR TREE
7. IN DYING MOMENTS – PART ONE
8. IN DYING MOMENTS – PART TWO
9. IN DYING MOMENTS – PART THREE
10. IN DYING MOMENTS – PART FOUR

IF HE CALLS HER

So, there he was
Walking down the street
Alone and lost he was
But with the whole world at his feet
And as he walked along
Contemplating his dreams
Little did he know
Everything was not as it seemed
Because at the tic of a clock

A slow-motion moment
Her eyes hit his
And a new era had begun
Awestruck he truly was
As two lives crossed paths
And they suddenly stopped walking
And when the second came ticking
They only left one trail

Now at first his mind was racing
Adrenalin pumping round
He could barely drive his car
He barely made a sound
Throughout their first encounters
His world was consumed with hers
He shared as many moments as he could with her
No excuse could ever be made
He soon became devoted

Motivated by her very essence
He knew his feelings were growing
And he knew he needed to control
But in all truth
He couldn't control it
As much as she couldn't control being beautiful

—

His heart was beginning to open
And soon he fell in love
The moments they shared were always his happiest
In her company he felt so relaxed
Time was timeless

He felt complete
When they did grow closer
After months of crazy thoughts
They shared so many fantastic moments
They were inspired together
They had happiness at last
Even for the briefest of moments
Unconditional love

It was such a beautiful thing
As the dust began to settle
And reality kicks in
The honeymoon was gone
And time hadn't kicked in

Despite the passion and despite the soul
Despite the heart
And the love they knew
Despite the pain
They knew what they had to do
And do it they did
With the blessing of each other
To rebuild their lives
And begin the testing
The testing of their passions
The testing of their love

As they walked out of each other's way
They wondered how long
Before they could finally enjoy their fate
Would they go back
To that beautiful place
They both once were
That is still negative

Future is unknown
For despite the love
Unconditional on his part
She has found happiness
Reason to depart
And as his tears rise
And his heart crumbles
He has to realize
And make a decision he does

He knows his intentions
Straight from his heart
But he also knows his illusions
He knows his control
He asks for her hand
And she cannot ride
Journey with him
Over the horizon

But she does love him
He sees her eyes twinkle
He hears the soul in her giggles
The beautiful dimples on her cheeks
He sees the softness of her skin
The gentleness of her touch
He sees the glow of her hair
As it whispers in the wind
He sees the joy of her company

The wonderful radiance she is
He sees the truth and depth of her heart
He sees what makes him complete
See every time he looks into her eyes
He wanders to a distant place

A place of love and a place of longing
He would love to see it
Just one more time
Give it one more shot

One last try
He knows she is smiling, and he knows she is fine
But he loves her ever so much
He wants to share another kiss
He wants to share the goosebumps
He wants to share the tears
He wants to share the laughter
He wants to share the hope
He wants to share his life
He wants to share every moment
He knows they both will love that
He knows they both deserve that
He knows that's where happily they can be

If he calls it
Will she hear
When he calls it
Will she come
Does he look out to the moon
And call out to his true love
Will she be whispering back
Before he has even begun

Will she open her heart to him
Will she accept him back
Will they ride off into the sunset
Even with just the clothes on their back
Will they hold hands again
Will they ever lay in each other's arms again

Will he ever know
Only she will
If she calls it
He will come
And if she doesn't
He needs to know

Because it is breaking his heart
And he knows not where to go
He asks her to steady his ship
Help show him which path to take
If just to let him heal
Only she can reveal
Only she can end
And stop this ordeal

BROKEN HEART

My name is Leon
And I have a broken heart
This is a new beginning
Where it is all going to start

If you have read my previous words
You will all see
That I was in love
And had thrown away the key

But it all went wrong
The curse had struck
The cracks appeared
We became unstuck

The candle had worn
The fire stopped burning
The sun had gone in
The darkness was returning

The moonlight was out
But no romance was scheduled
The spark that once was
Could no longer be peddled

We had plunged into the darkness
Only one of us would emerge
And that would be me
My soul in a hearse

Carry me away
Let me sink to the depths
I cannot take this anymore
It is too hard to accept

To express my emotions
I would need a few days
But read on for the start
It is called 'middle of a maze'

This maze represents
The ill fate of my being
My heart is the center
And believed it was winning

But this maze is different
The center is the start
You have to find your way out
Believe you can depart

Its every pathway
Its very design
Is based on emotions
A twisted grapevine

In the core is where I am
I have been placed in the middle
And for every corner I try to turn
I am presented with a riddle

And to solve that riddle
I have to understand
That my relationship is over
She has forced my hand

I have to force my way out
Of this self-destructive faze
Put an end to these emotions
Escape from the maze

So I will take my heart
Now so humble and sore
I will break it in half
I accept it is no more

The broken heart
So sad and lonely
A harsh maze ahead
A perilous journey

Journey I must
Or make myself ill
Get up and try
For there is hope still

HAPPINESS

Pain ravages my body
Eating at my heart
Against all belief
I find us apart

My existence belittled
My personality not entertained
The smiles I had created
No longer had my love gained

Complications would arise
From day one I knew
But true love is such
That we would pull through

I felt we were strong
United as one
We seemed unbeatable
Never would we run

Us against the world
The usual cliché
But for all its worth
It was our forte

We were in love
Our passion a fever
We had our moments
And always found either

A future so bright
Dreams and fantasies
Slowly forming
Becoming reality

Marriage and children
Our dream home
There were no limits
To how far we would roam

However, we were naïve
To developments around us
A family discontent
Out to destroy us

Dirty tricks
Lies and deceit
Never was I accepted
Always at their feet

We let down our guard
We shared our emotion
In the midst
There was downfall in motion

Ammunition sprung
From the jaws of our oppressor
It struck us down
Our love became inferior

You instantly forgot
Our colorful past
For fear and respect
You took down our mast

You joined their ranks
And turned against me
No longer a future
No longer were we

You were confused
But made clear your loyalty
Those were their intentions
An end to our royalty

Forgotten was your smile
Our endless glory
So quickly surrendered
The end to our story

How can love
Be so quickly abused
No longer defended
No longer pursued

Our bond was broken
My life at an end
My emotion crushed
Nothing to extend

Nothing to hope for
Nothing to reach
No longer a heart
My soul had been breached

Your refusal to honor
Our love of so long
Your refusal to honor
The star to which we belong

You let them kill us
You punished me well
So much for love
I am in hell

Judged on principals
Judged on moral
My heart stands for nothing
Banished...in peril

The waves of pain
Will never leave me
The hurt of your defection
So hard to forgive

I cannot understand
Why you fear their aggression
I would die a martyr for you
There would be no question

If you loved me
You would feel the same
Obviously not
You feel no pain

I am now the outcast
And will always be blamed
Now I have to live
A life with no flame

I once wrote of you
To spread light rife
Where did that go
Where was your fight

Where is your heart
Your desire of me
Where was the need
For peace and harmony

Try as I might
I will always be bad
I will always inspire hate
I am simply a man

I came out of my box
And I found you
But now I go back
Loneliness will ensue

My heart bleeds angel
I wish for life
To treat me kinder
Anything nice

But love is gone
Out of the question
Defeated by you
And a life of suppression

They have destroyed me
And you did not help
Thank you, sweet angel
Think of yourself

Don't think for me
For I am dead
Back in the box
A dark road ahead

I cry in vain
Tears of sadness
My soul mate has left me
So much for happiness

HEARTBREAKER

This very moment in time
An end to a fourth day
Of torment and pertinence
Can my feelings be tamed

Feelings for my heart, ripped from my soul
Feelings for my twin, now turned cold
Emotions now pouring, and crying with repent
A year of true passion, that is dead with no end

A year in four days
That's what it has become
A year of true friendship
Emotion and soul

A flame of two souls
Once benevolent, now castigated
Once so rosy, now so weak
In all events hold lies and deceit

Burning desire for which only hurt prevails
Spite and ransom, blame and self-pity
Ignorance and deception
No seeds of infinity

A year in four days
And in four days it is gone
In four days
It wanders the streets

The friendship wanders
Alone in the world
Isolated in the world
And as the wind blows it soars like a plane
Gliding in the wind

Once all mighty, strong and powerful
It is now so light, and blemished as such
As it rises and falls, it finds no home
It finds no attraction, no love of its own

This friendship is dead
Never to return
For in lies and deceit
No flame will ever burn

I knew a wonderful female once
True in every way
Once amazing to talk to and easy to love

I could open my heart and release tremendous secrets
I could touch on life, and liberate my mind
I could vilify evil and peruse my dreams
With a friend of celestial nature, with a wonderful mind

We spoke for hours, spent days in the sun
Laughed and cried together and bore strength as one
We spoke our hearts and our hearts spoke advice
We preached and we listened, loved and enticed

True friends we were
Soul mates for life
But now for it to end
Destroyed in strife

Hurt, pain
Strong words
Words that engulf me like flames to dry trees
They take hold of my body
And encircle my heart

A friendship of joy, belief and true wanting
Ended in agony, vengeance and venom
It hurts beyond belief
The crime, the complexity

—

The placid nature of the words
Be gone your banished
No longer heard

The headline alone commanding so much anger and bitterness
You have ruined my life
You have ruined my life
Five words bringing tears to my eyes

How…Why…

Love, honor, passion and trust
Strong words
Words that were spoken
But never so silently
Never explored
Just adopted and isolated

And they presented themselves to two souls
Yet somehow, they grew cold
But the feeling is still there
And they cannot forget
The dream of love
And when they first met

The headline alone commanding so much intensity and brilliance
I love you
I love you
Three words bringing tears to my eyes
Where have they gone
Why not told
Where have they gone…how…why…

Is this a premonition or is it just words
Can I predict the comparison in two hearts
The identity and flow, truth and certainty
That cannot be manipulated, tried and forgot

So please may I, the scapegoat of this war
Join in peace, and follow in awe
Awe of what is true
Awe of what is there
That cannot be denied

I can only stare
Stare into the future
And feel two dreams
Collaborate and remember
Where passion does stream

And where the existence falls, I do not know
Where the friendship falls, I do not know
Both are gliding
Rising and falling
Whilst we are all innocent victims
Angry and foreboding

I cannot bear to comprehend the fear of her love
I cannot bear to comprehend his hurt and his pain
And I cannot bear to comprehend, my own ruin
distress and upset

So many questions, so many endless thoughts
Her passion for life and his severely tested
But then all was tried
And all was ended

Read between the lines
Learn from the mistakes
Believe in my message
For that is all it will take

If you believe in the evidence
Happiness will prevail
Love shall be the winner
Not this tragic tale

INSANE

The world spins and the world turns
I live in a place where nothing feels right
Tears stream down my face like a waterfall
I try to choke back but I can't seem to fight
I try to do what's best, but it never seems to work
I try to believe that one day it will happen
The day is yet to come, and I've given up being patient
What good is patience with no strength and resolve

It always seems to rain, and I want to get dry
When it all seems too much, I've always tried
I've thought about what I want, what it could possibly take
I can never work it out through the endless mistakes
Whatever it is it is never is enough
Could it be love or could it be material
It is yet to come to me, and I have already lost faith
I know it sounds selfish, but I can no longer pursue this dream

My patience has worn thin and my heart wants to give up
What is this life because I want to know
I live in a world that feels so insane
Maybe I should go and end it right now

It seems like the only path left to take
I know I have no right to take my time for granted
I was given a gift to breathe the air of life
But darkness is there, so tempting it seems

What else could there be to stop this pain
I can't question anymore
I don't feel any hope
I won't wait anymore on a shattered dream

—

Everything I have longed for has failed to come
When I have acted on a moment it always runs
Slips through my grasp
It is all too much
I can't find a way out

I know the darkness answers
An exit from this world
A place with no direction and thoughts to disturb
What does this world offer
But endless time infused with pain
There is only one way to go
Or I will end up insane

THE BIRDS FROM OUR TREE

Do we think sad thoughts
Do we believe in misery
Are we destined to believe
In suffering and repress
Why do we live on such callous design
On such a dire state of mystery
That our lives come to an end
And happiness is too distant

When friendships form
And come to an end
When love becomes a word
And comes to an end
When we join in delight
It comes to an end
Yet we wonder why
Our minds seek dire

We wonder and stare
Why we feel so low
Why life is not living
And why it does not flow
It does not flow
It does not stream
It just hits a block
Tension and we are powerless

A verbal negative
Everything is against
Why do we live for such relative confrontation
And why do we believe in constant fixation
We want to oppress and negotiate power
But we want to be loved and cherished in honor
We long for the dream,
Of the beach and sea

Wishing for love
The soul redeems
We long for the stars
The night of romance
We live it so distant
But it's our existence

Its candle stands tall
It will not burn, and it will not fall
We cannot pass or move
We are trapped in a world of our mind and its own
May we only attempt to prevail

Love makes no sense
People betray us
We believe in their wonder and fall for their charm
We believe in their soul and they can do no wrong
They are ecstasy, they make our hearts burn
Eager anticipation and wanting will follow
And we allow for hurt

They may have chances, for we are now wrong
We don't have devotion, but they are still special
We don't have ill feeling but only disillusion
They watch for our joy
And feed on our wanting
They feel good for watching us suffer
Suffer in pain and time that will pass
And they flatter excuses
Thick and too fast
And again, they charm
And again, they call
We need to wake, we need to wake

Will we live for them and allow no life
No life for ourselves, but just for them
But they are not there
Not in heart
Not in soul
We are still empty, and we are still cold

———

75

We are stuck between four walls
And there is no window
We wait and we wait for the end
Our burning desire burns slower and slower, colder and colder
Why do they not want
Why don't they burn

And in my space, I feel a tree
It stands tall and strong and I know it's my own
Filled with flower and filled with joy
My tree held love and life as a ploy
It housed our creature and it housed our birds
It housed our fixation
And our admiration in words

But as they mistreat and as they do wrong
Our tree begins to empty
And we start to feel wrong
The birds fly far
Our lives are not strong
We fail to wonder
Why we are not wanted
We fall to our knees
And keep wondering why
Wondering why, we have fallen to a knee
Wondering why the birds still don't return
To our ailing love tree

I do write from heart and I do write from soul
I want you to feel and I want you to see
Don't be like me and always believe
Your birds will come back
And bring life to your tree

76

IN DYING MOMENTS – PART ONE

It's easy to look back on my life and plead sympathy
I had a crap school
No friends and no family
No life outside
I was inside the box
No coming out
Leave me to rot
I don't want your insults
Your views or your world
I don't want your opinion
Your wife or your girl
All I want from you God
Is true love and harmony
You give me that
And I will always plead mercy
Mercy to you
For making me smile
Mercy to you
For making it worth while
You made me work hard
It was a struggle
Mental torture
Trapped in a bubble
I couldn't get out
I couldn't get away
All I could do
Was fear the next day
Some evil prick
Wants it to burst
Wants to ruin me
As if I'm a curse
They want to destroy me
But I will respond
Rise to the sky
The universe and beyond
The whole point of me
Is love in its glory

Soul mates and heartbeats
Together as one
That's what I crave
And all I ask
That's what I now have
And I take off the mask
A mask scarred by bullies
Rapists and murderers
Hurt and corruption
Need I go further
Do you want to hear
Of all the names
Do you want to hear
Of a childhood of shame
Read on for part two
We will go on a journey
Just me and you

IN DYING MOMENTS – PART TWO

This part is the memory
Of me when I was a child
One day at my primary
A day I will always revile
Here it proceeds
Please do not cry for me
I am writing this for a reason
And it is not for sympathy
The reason will come clear
When my hand stops typing
But for now, this is my tapestry
Laid out in writing

Casts on both legs
A disease of the hips
I had a stick in between
Careful, don't trip
If you fall down
You won't get up
No one can help
You idiot you're stuck!

Exclamation mark yep
It is harmless banter
At first, it's a joke
You learn to cope
But when you're surrounded
With nowhere to go
Suddenly it's over
You get a lump in your throat

Here it comes
The fatal push
You're powerless now
Deep in the bush
I couldn't get up
I had no support
Nothing to clasp

Sorry, you've been caught
Your times up
Or rather the clocks ticking
Whatever way you see it
You're stuck
You can't fucking get up
You're a helpless piece of shit
Sorry mate, hard luck

Shall I move on
Enter dying moments
Are you sure you want to know, every component
Ok now you're ready
If you're sure here it goes
Here's a story, to keep you on your toes
Roll on part three
Can this be any more morose

IN DYING MOMENTS – PART THREE

Think of an alley
Dark and rough
Cold and squalid
Damp and enclosed
Quiet and far
From human ears
Perfect for vandals
And enticing fear
Strangers wander
With the occasional glance
Vandals surpass
With graffiti and trance
Trance of drugs
Their lives are gone
Lost in a spiral
Forever alone

And in that alley
Suddenly noise erupted
Fear had been enticed
Quiet disrupted
Four men and a female
Screaming irony
Four voices of excitement
One of tyranny
A loud crash
As the female falls
Onto sprawled rubbish
She tries to crawl
She scratches the wall
Her world is surrounded
The wall is cold
Her heart stops pounding

They keep on touching
Gripping and scrapping
Groping and hitting
Dragging and spitting
One hand on mouth
Another on bare chest
Another on leg
And yet another on chest
Another pulls and grapples
Another shreds
Another digs
And yet another on chest
Clothes all ripped
Their invasion gets intense
She kicks and fights
But she is fast losing strength
She cannot continue
Her heart is dying
For all her fighting
Her only produce is crying

They fend off her clothes
And now she is bare
Natural one says
Isn't she fair
They slowly succumb
To their violent lust
One infiltrates
And for the rest it's a must
Some get ready
Others hold her down
They all want a chance
To gain a sick crown
She lies there naked
Helpless and overpowered
While they now fight
They still won't spare her

One by one
They invade her body
Piercing her soul
Disgust and melancholy
Poignant is the disgrace
Her soul cannot escape
Incursion it suffers
Stunning hurt is her fate
In her closing moments of life
Agony is her only memory
Her final emotion
In lasting eternity
Merciless increments
Revulsion and repugnance
Repellent afflicts
In dying moments

Shouting and screaming
A great victory
One more to go
Another sick adversary
They are now done
But still want to feel
Still no end
To her horrific ordeal
They spit and kick now, clearly wanting blood
They now want to hurt, with blows and thuds
One still infiltrates, now a sickening object
And she writhed in agony, a terrifying effect
She is starting to bleed
Her face jarred with pain
They continue to blow
Fucking insane
They laugh and scream
Shout a sick ritual
Kings of sick torture
Souls uninhabitable

She cannot scream
Her throat choked with blood
Chest soaked with intrusions
She can hardly breathe
Legs and arms
Scratched and cut
Drenched with her ordeal
Of monstrous glut
Her mind no longer sane
Crushed and abused
Her world no longer there
Gone into recluse
Waves of anguish
Distress and misery
She no longer moves
Her senses derisory

She cannot fight
She has no world
She has been broken
Slammed and hurled
Used
Abused
Battered
Shattered
Innocence gone
Her life betrayed
Sanity and soul
Raped and taken away

IN DYING MOMENTS – PART FOUR

I watch
I cannot help
Shocked, I cannot move
My heart is broken
My head pounding with hurt
I felt the pain
The evil and hatred

Memories forever
Never to leave
These images of anguish and suffering
I am always to see
They build up inside me
And into a dream
A dream of my destiny
The dream tells of my ending
Tells of my death
The only sense
I can make of this world
Is that vision of fate
In which my dream unfurls

Slowly there is pain
Seeping through my veins
I am finding it hard to breathe
My lungs feel no gain
I cry and I hurt
My heart turns blind
I cannot feel
I cannot see
My soul is so cold
In moments like these
As the light starts to form
I know of my passage
My transition from this life
And into a new world
Before I go
Remember this is still my dream

I recite my last emotion
I present it with frightening ease
The following is my final prayer
My ending contribution
Keep on reading
My personal retribution

I will die with the hatred, disgust and repulsion
I'm not good enough for love, in my happiness there's expulsion
I do not see this world
I see no time
I see no life
Welcome unkind
I was born into a world of where I do not feel a pulse
Square peg, round hole, can you make it correspond
I have so many bad dreams
So many terrible thoughts
I cannot explain it
Or change my due course

I will always see
These malevolent memories
I will always see
These treacherous life components
Forever they bear torture
A perfidious rodent
Always my life
In dying moments

CHAPTER FOUR

WOKEN

Six long years had passed, and I hadn't written a single word. I felt the writing stage of my life was over but those who have suffered heartbreak know how it can lead to other demons into your life. Past memories and insecurities come out to tease and haunt you. Like many young men I tried to ignore the shock and pain and 'move on'. But, deep down I had no inspiration, no hope and no desire. My existence was like a desolate wasteland. I had been under this dark spell for so long that I felt the voices were permanently silenced but as I aimlessly drifted from place to place, life threw me a second chance. I was in my mid-twenties with not much to show but a pile of debt and a rented flat. Little did I know that my years of suffering were about to be over. I was struck, quite 'out of the blue' when love decided to come for me again. With it the voices remerged with raging positivity as my heart was preparing to be repaired. I was in overdrive and the words were coming at a million miles an hour. That's the funny thing about life; its fragility and instability can lead to its very beauty.

These 12 poems express my journey into *recovery*:

1. HOPE
2. OFF WITH THE MASK
3. WHAT DO YOU SEE
4. WHAT COURSE
5. BOUNCE
6. DAYDREAM
7. US
8. FLY
9. DAZE
10. ONE
11. RHYMES AND RHYTHMS
12. BLUE TOUCH PAPER

—

HOPE

Have you ever felt the emptiness
The desolate self-belief
Have you ever been to a place
Where your life has become aimless
No goals or objectives
No will to soldier on
No desire to achieve
All your passion gone
Have you ever been so tired
Of picking yourself off the ground
Have you felt like giving up
Like you're wandering into oblivion

Have you started to ask yourself the question
What have you done to the world
Why must you draw the short straw
Why must you stay positive
What have you ever done
To deserve this endless misery
With no light at the end of the tunnel
And all of your energy consumed
The only option left
Is the one you have always longed for
But blocked in the back of your mind
Be strong you have said
Happiness will prevail

Keep picking yourself up
This is just the test of life
Everyone goes through this
You will make it in the end
Stop thinking so negatively
One day all will be well
Well you have thought those thoughts
A million times over

You have been to happy places
Only for it always to be taken away
Who can understand
When will it ever end
I cannot suffer yet more heartache
Or I will have no heart left

For all of you out there for which this poem can relate
There is someone here who hears you
And I promise that it will end
But it will not end as you think
With your heart no longer beating
Your story will become a happy one
As the balance of life prevails
The sun will end up shining
And for once your smiles will be true
The front you put up will disappear
And your true colors will shine through
Be patient my friends
Always keep your faith

Celebrate your life and engage your soul
At the end of the road you will find happiness
Not an end to your life as you have believed
Banish those thoughts and challenge your mind
Embrace a wondrous spirit and fight for your right
Your right to your happiness and right to your smile
Life is precious
Live every day as if it's your last
Follow your heart and achieve your ambitions
Do not regret a moment
Stay true to yourself
Be positive
Believe in your soul
And let fate take care of the rest

OFF WITH THE MASK

And here I am
All alone
You see me staring
At a wall of stone
I stand and watch
And think of my life
Ponder my future
Alienate strife
For all is good
I'm living in sunshine
I have true love
And the beauty of time
Yes, life is good
It sure is fine
Preach to the sky
Yes, she is mine
As we stroll through the fields
Hands locked tight
The sun beams down
On a moment so bright
I cannot present
My undying love
Love cannot be explained
Written or trained
It can only be expressed
And judged by the world
Actions speak louder
Than words will ever tell
Off with the mask
Oh, how I love her
Now and forever
God it is so true

WHAT DO YOU SEE

Long distance
Is turbulence
I feel like I long to be
To be a man
To be a viper
To be a sniper
To be much kinder
To feel like you belong to me
I could eat chopped liver
Just to shiver
At what you mean to me
Your longing
Your wanting
All there is to see
See as I am looking out
I stomp and shout
At what you mean to me
And I feel it is working
All the work I am shirking
Just for time for us
To work hard enough
Just so we can be free
See what this is to me
Like looking out to sea
Is a place for you and me
Do you watch from the shadows
Do you see it burning
The want
The hurting
For me to stop staring
The weakness is killing me
I want this to be working
I will never stop working
See all I want is you

Never will we be through
For while I'm always breathing
I will never stop believing
Never stop dreaming
Watching from the ceiling
The height from above
Soaring like a dove
Can never get enough
And all I really want is you
I will never stop caring
Never stop daring
You are always dazzling
Watching and smiling
Looking so stunning
Melting my cunning
My innermost being
Defenses and ceilings
You wash them all away
What can I say
Starting today
I am going to hold your heart
And let us start
This poetry in motion
Because that is where we are going
To a place where we will stay
Because today is the day
We are going away
Wandering the oasis
On a daily basis
I cannot believe my luck
I've come unstuck
Mentally unstable
I can't seem to contain
This wonder that you show
That always seems to grow
I can't seem to shake
These emotions that you make
You always seem to make me
So very happy
My heart goes crazy

Then I say maybe
Maybe there is justice
Maybe there is gold
Maybe there is silver
To have and to hold
Whisper in your ear
Melt every fear
Work towards the start
Of day number two
Of just me and you
Hear these words
Forget the curse
Of always going wrong
Never being strong
Not done now
Not alone
On a throne
On a pedestal
Waxing lyrical
Blindly hysterical
Can't believe my luck
It is driving me nuts
Like I've won the lottery
Solved the mystery
Must be a conspiracy
What happened with you and me
Broke the mould
Hit it stone cold
Shadowed by the light
Shining so bright
Shielded from the rays
Oh, my days
How did we not see
The thing with you and me
Ignoring life
Forgetting the strife
Feeling the spice
Being so nice
Laying down the natural
Wandering around

94

Barely making a sound
We might as well as whisper
Shadows beneath the wind
I want to shout
I want to be heard
But my voice is frozen
Stunned and speechless
When you just gave me
Our first kiss
You got me at zero
Never had a chance to get off the mark
Your heart had spoken
I had awoken
And there you were
Standing in front of me
You were all that I could see
Then we became you and me
This is my eulogy
This is my sound
You are all sound
Wrapped in a blanket
I can feel it, I can taste it
Your warmth and your smile
It has taken a while
But here we are again
Me with a pen
You with the words
Hearing the next verse
Chapter new
Just me and you
Signing off I am out
But I am still about
I am not leaving you
Just going for a while
Please lend me your smile
I promise I will bring it back soon
I will be watching the moon
Staring at the same spot
Watching till I drop
And as I fall

I begin to start dreaming
And I never stop believing
In faith in you and me
I just want you to see
Me and you baby
All the way you will see
Out
Shout
Just you and me

WHAT COURSE

I've arrived
On the fringe
People looking in
I'm noticed
Challenged
Multi task zone

I'm home
I'm here
Never ever fear
I will hold you so dear
Ever in time
Beating my chest
Never allowing rest
Time to invest
In the things we like the most
We don't have toast
We might have a roast
Memories like ghosts
Of past present and future
Things that make me laugh
Blasts from the past
Oceans drawing in
Twinkling under the stars
Cars and road trips
Always a time
Being prone to a slip
A trip or a fall
Or whatever it's called
I will stand up
And shrug it all off

On the go
Never slow
Giving it a try
Never being shy
I won't hold back
I am back

I'm here
In the flesh
Put me to the test
I will soar through the air
With my feet right on the ground

My mind surveys the future
Calculating the risks
Adding up the numbers
Anticipating the rhymes
Or the times
Whatever
Just trying to be clever
Got to watch my ego
I will watch it
Own it
Want to outgrow it
I will always let you hold it
And keep me in tow
I will listen to you
Consider you
Never give up for you
I want you
I need you
Forever in time
Holding hands
Making that stand
Planning our dreams
Our realities and time

But I will wake up each day
And always say
I love you always
Please never go away
I want you to stay
To play and to relay
My feelings straight back at me
Pulling at my strings
The chords
The sounds

You can hear a penny drop
The gravity of the beating heart
Pounding in your mind

And there you are
Causing a stir
Prickling my nerves
To the beat of my heart
And I stir and awaken
Adrenaline growing rampant
I glisten at your touch
Your warmth and your stuff
The things of your dreams
Your baggage's and screams
Your wants and your desires
Deafening it seems
As I begin to imagine
The connection we have
I can't help but wonder
Of what hopes we have
Admire at our destiny
Wonder at our dreams
Elated by your touch
Dazed by your mind

I started the day strong
Then I thought of a song
After gazing at your picture
Your smile is such a winner
Your voice and all of your drama
The moments and the karma
You will soon be at my side
Continuing our ride
Emotions always high
We want and we deliver
We calculate our next move

We are both strong
We are both sound
Beating our chests
But not too hard mind
I'm joking
Cracking
Laughing and debating
Wondering
Dreaming
Lost in my mind
I look at you
I look at us
Can't believe
I caught such luck
Or maybe not
I was destined for the lot
I guess I will never know
Wind rain or snow
All I know
Is that I am there
Looking back from that picture
Humming that song
Snapped in a moment
Locked in time
In between the frame
Protrudes the hopes of two lovers
Star gazers
Love makers
Beaming a true smile
One from the heart
To never be forgot
The still of a moment
You will never forget
You break out of the fantasy
Double check the reality
Remember where we were
Do you remember this
Do you recall that
Oh yea remember this
So funny what it was

So wonderful that it felt
So amazing that this was
Such glory through the glass
It catches the light
The picture frame that is
All of a sudden so bright
The scene now becomes
It announces itself
That snap shot of time
Looks at me and says
You will always be mine
And I will always be yours
As long as you will have me of course

First second or third
Starters main or dessert
Which one shall we have
Where shall we go
You are here and so am I
So what journey now should we ride
How will we do it
Where are we going to go
No matter where
No matter what
Hold my hand
Because we won't stop
Every day
What do you say
Let's go and stay
One step ahead of time

You will be mine
I will be yours
Can't wait for the tour
The details
The course
I'm going to go for the starter
The food on a platter
Might have two
Why ever not

What have we got to lose
But for a few moments in time
I don't take it for granted
And never will I do
But for just me and you
We have millions more
We won it
The jackpot
And we are just right here
Soaring through the jet stream
Of our never-ending thoughts
Are the visions
Of you and me
And love of course

I am ready to do this
I guess is what I mean
Let me just say sorry
It never happened from the beginning
Forgive me
And hold me
Let's replay the story
Ignore me
I'm being silly
It's just a photograph
But listen to me
It makes me think
I guess I'm trying to say
I love you in every way
You challenge me
Pressure me
Light between you and me
You make me see
The rights and wrongs
The things I've done
Perspective in one
That's what I do
Think of me and you
I think of all these things
My mind can never win

Rule over my heart
I don't think so
Go
Get out of it
You won't change my mind
But if that is the case
Then so be it
Going to risk it
For a chocolate biscuit
Sacrifice the craziness
Of chocolate digestives
The crave and the wanting
The sudden desire
It won't be arisen
Thanks in kind

I will risk it
For just one beat
Of the drum of my heart
In the base
Of the sound of drums
The ticking
The second
Actually, the split second
The moment it takes
To expand and contract
Right in that moment
I will expose it
Unleash it
My decision
To let my heart rule my head
And when I did it
I gave myself unto you
I told you
I was going to
Give you all of me
All of me

Such an inspirational voice
So sure, it was based
On a dream about
Someone like you
Now there is a song
That will always ring true
From a glorious voice
An artist of visions
One of the greatest of all time
The best there was
The best there is
But still is not as good
As my mistress

Haha
So funny
The rumble of your tummy
Hehe I can't believe it
Such thoughts from a picture
It really is funny
My mind is running away with me
I'm so sorry for rambling
But I'm gushing and floating
Gloating and exposing
What you draw from my mind
You take it
Repaint it
And then tell me I'm fine
I'm fine
I'm thin
I'm crisp
Folded
Noted
Corrected
Neat and tidy
I'm good
Looking good
Clean shaved
Displayed
Awed and admired

Ok maybe not admired
But not yet
Just wait for it
Open it and read it
Notice it
Know it
That is where it is
The want and desire
The want to be admired
The emotions that you think
The ones you write in ink
That is what this is
That I'm blurting out on paper
Actually, that's a lie
I've got an app for that
And that's that
The ramblings
The words
The freestyle
Just the voice of an old man

Haha
I am
Or I'm not
Who knows
It's just a number anyway
But anyway
Just saying
Just writing and playing
Tennis with my mind
My work and my life
Back and forth
We go and go
Drifting
Calming
Quietening
Not calling
Just thinking
Whispering
Alternatively speaking

I'm just going away
Thinking for another day
The day will come
When we read or listen to this one
And the next one
And all I've done
All I've become
With our course set as one

BOUNCE

What do I have to do
Do I leave in the shadows tonight
Where do I have to go
Do I walk right into the light
Do I leave you to love me
Do I let you put it right
Do I wander into the wind
With you right by my side
Always holding my hand
Wandering what is the plan
Always believing
While we drift right through this land

I don't want you to be hurting
Never want you to be sad
I only want smiling and laughter
Always holding my hand
Show me how to want you
How to let myself go
Following my spirit
Dragging my heart in tow
Do I keep you near me
Feel the warmth of your skin
Stand shoulder to shoulder
Arm in arm
Walk the same footsteps
Dream the same dream

I feel weak and cold
When I whisper in my ear
Shall I let myself go
Succumb to my fear
Let it beat me
As you draw near
Catching my breath
Holding my tears
I want to let you in
Let true love win

Give it a second chance
Take happiness for a spin
You inspire my smiles
Massage my mind
Keeping your love
So wonderful and kind
As I break the barrier
And give myself to you
I whisper the words
So beautiful and true
I love you
I'm done being sad
I want you like crazy
It is driving me mad
I am sorry I have hurt you
What I have put you through
From now on baby
It is just me and you

The oceans of mars
Simply melted away
Left a bed of dust
A ball of warm rock
No atmosphere to speak of
No life to observe
Wandering lost
In this great universe
But when it works
This journey of fate
You look out across
To the earth in its glory
Twinkling beneath the stars
A beacon of blue
I can often compare it
To what I think of you
Full of energy
Burning through as light
Beaming ecstasy
Shining so bright
One in a trillion

That is what you are
Jumped right over the hurdles
Always setting a bar
A bar of how
To live this life
How to be free
How to be nice
How I want you
As I write these lines now
Lean right over to you
And give you a kiss

Watch you giggle
As your cheeks blush
I'm starting to gush
What a rush
Never too much
I will treat you as such
My mind is now mush
Time for me to wrap up
Chapter four
Right out of the front door
Chapter five
Next in line
What to expect
From this wonderful love fest

Feast your eyes on us
Our passionate lust
Rising from the dust
Springing into bloom
Forgetting the gloom
Becoming a resident
In a world that is heaven sent
Green and blue
With clouds of white
Spinning beneath the sun
So gold and yellow
Always staring at one another
Dodging the other planets

Our eyes never parting
Our warmth never slacking
Our private galaxy of nothing
But we are something
What do I do
Now I have found you
And you have found me

Well I guess I will just stay here
Live without any fear
Wherever we go
I will always be close
It is time to go now
Time to make the most
Vacate this post

Let's go for it
Let's feel it
Let's caress it
Let's do it
Let's take it
Let's want it
Let's journey
Let's bounce

DAYDREAM

As I close my eyes
I remind myself of the good times
The bad times
The lost times

All around me
All I can see
Are little white traces
Of just you and me
I've changed my life
I've started a new reign
Starting today I have realized
That there can be a grain
A crumb of small comfort
Microbe of sand
Always shall I know
Of how much there is to have

Life is so precious
Special in every way
And all I can think about
Is you everyday
From darkness to light
Comes hope and applause
For I am about to declare
That I am forever yours
The journey we have travelled
So far and so wide
Never does it faze me
Or kick me offside
In my mind I know
It is all I can see
Make no mistake
This is just about you and me

Your smile and your dimple
Your body and your warmth
Your mind and your soul
Your comfort and laughter
Your giggle and your shivers
Always makes me quiver
I shudder at the thought
Of your breath on my neck
I shake at the touch
Of your heart on my chest
We wander in spirit
Joined hand in hand
Floating along the breeze
Drifting in the sand
Listening to the beach waves
Lapping in the distance
When we are together
The only two in existence

We are the clouds
Floating in the sky
Reaching out for sunrise
Watching the storm clouds float by
Whatever the weather
The drama or our friends
All of the life we are building
Forever I will defend
I will always fight
For what I believe in
And just so you know
I believe in you

The world is a battlefield
With life as its conscience
I stand before you
To defend your honor
I will be brave
I will be strong
I will cover you in goosebumps
Forever long

You have been saying
I love you
Well I say back
I love you long time
I can make a joke
From those five words
But the irony is
I could write a verse
I could write a chorus
I could write a song
My passion to write
Has been reborn
You have softened my pain
Turned it to mush
Run amok through my mind
Made me gush
I am stunned by the impact
Of your wonderful being
Tearful of life
For the joy you bring

Flowing faster now
My heart is racing
As I slide through these words
I think I should start pacing
But you get me all fuzzy
Crazy inside
You have no idea
How you have lightened my life
As lump in my throat
Is now starting to form
My eyes are dry
My arms are shaking
My mind is slow
My hands are aching

I have just noticed
That you are not around
That cloud I was floating on
Had sent me to ground
I guess I should go now
But that lump is getting bigger
I don't want to leave you
In this moment so sincere

I feel like by doing this
You are right here next to me
I feel like I'm talking to you
Connecting mid-stream
Equilibrium is amazing
We have joined through our karma
I can sense you around me
Shining through armour
Your gust and your guile
Strength to beguile
Your wondrous person
Your beautiful smile

I am going to go now
This daydream is nearly over
We will wait until next time
For the next instalment of this chapter
I am just going to turn the page
I will be back in a hurry
I would give but everything
To again feel that flurry
That flutter in my heart
That I touched on before
I will be back
For a beautiful encore

US

I need to explain
To write down in words
The meaning of events
That have inspired this chapter
See it started at Christmas
With a letter through a door
A moment of faith
Something that meant more
All was slow
Until that one day
My whole life changed
In every single way
Were things beautiful at first
Were we working as one
Soon I realized
It was not that fun
I felt so controlled
Suffocated and used
I knew we were struggling
Blown our spark, our fuse
Like the stars in the sky
We were miles apart
Living a routine
Right from the start
She erased my history
I was ashamed of my past
She dominated my life
My smile would never last
I often wondered
If my life could be stronger
Often considered
If I could handle much longer
Throughout my life
I have always believed
Dreamt of women
Pursued that dream
All of my thoughts
My faith and ideology

Ripped from my heart
And replaced with an effigy
An effigy of hurt
Pain and deceit
The problem is
I never got a receipt
I cannot take it back
Return all of those feelings
I placed a cover over my heart
For it has reached a ceiling
A dizzy height
Where it almost fell off
I had enough
Took my snout from the trough
The truth is I was greedy
I wanted it all
I took the wrong path
I was set up for a fall
Despite my weakness
My fear of resentment
I addressed my concerns
Gave my heart treatment
I suffered the tears
The distress and the drama
Told myself to hold out
For soon there would be karma
I knew it would be hard
To watch her move on
I had to stay strong
Envisage her gone
As she walked from my life
A weight was lifted
I felt so much lighter
Enlightened
Gifted

The power of life
The irony of happiness
I pondered my journey
Riddled with sadness
When I say my soul is lost
She was not the cause
The truth of it all is
I had never changed course
I was on a road to nothing
A complete dead end
Wandering the world
Denying a trend

The trend of a smile
So passionate and bright
The dazzling aurora
That has set me alight
Throughout all of this time
You were staring straight ahead
All of this time
All of these words were unsaid
We had a connection
That has survived for so long
Even in Boston
We were always so strong
Yet we did not know it
But it was right there
My eyesight is bad
I thought the road was bare
I could not see you
Shining in the distance
So radiant and dazzling
Your smile so constant
When you sent me that message
It was a spark on my soul
I knew there was something
A story untold
I wanted to write
About the journey so far
I wanted to define

Our hearts in a jar
Because we have connected
Both you and I
Our bubble has wandered
Soared through the sky
We have always been inspired
Dazzled and lifted
I have always believed
You are so wonderful and gifted
Your smile and your laugh
The way you play with your hair
The hundreds of earrings
Dangling in the air
The warmth of your touch
The passion of your embrace
Your spirit and nature
Your natural grace

I wander the darkness
Forlorn to your wake
For you are so beautiful
In every step you take
Your mind strong and bold
I want you so much
Your dream holds my soul
And I cherish your touch
For you touch me in heart
And you touch me in mind
I want you to know
You always to be mine

Life throws you diamonds
And there is too many to hold
You cannot have them all
Your heart must be bold
You must pick one
From the sparkling rainfall
Stick by that choice
And joy will prevail
If that diamond chooses to leave

From your gentle grasp
Allow it to wander
But do not let it last
It must be your goal
To your dyeing days
To stand by your diamond
As it shines in every way
It is the twinkle in your eye
The skip in your step
Bear it your soul
And let heaven protect
Declare your heart
And feel the vibe
It may not work
But you can always try

Time is too slow, for those who wait
It is too swift, for those who fear
It can be too long, for those who grieve
And is always too short, for those who rejoice
But it is a fact, that for those who love
Our wonderful time, will be a blissful eternity

We will take a slow walk
On this eternity I write of
Watch out for the obstacles
Haunting us both
Simplify the process
Shut all the doors
Strip it back
So it's just mine and yours

Let your heart guide you
It whispers so listen closely
I will say this once
So read it slowly
I will not walk away
Or let you down
You will always be able
To have me around
I believe in you
In all that there is
I will always show you
Every time we kiss
When we embrace
I will transfer that faith
Hold you so close
Till my muscles start to ache
We will take things slowly
Admire the view
But one thing is for sure
All I want is you

FLY

If I could
Be able to fly
I don't know why
I'm thinking of this today
It is strange
In a way
That this is on my mind
But if I could fly
Wouldn't I at least try
To change the landscape
And fly on by
So I was wandering
All about it
And I thought of you
And that's all there was to it
And onwards I flew

I let my mind wander
So there we are
One day in the future
The sun is blazing
We are amazing
Soaring to the stars
Married in honor
Forever my lover
A house in the bag
And cars on the road
Nice things
Maybe a pet
Kids on the way
That's a sure bet
We have it all

All these things
And all the while
I'm just wandering
If this were it
And if we could do
Wouldn't we fly
Wouldn't you

Let us soar
Race past the rain
Pierce the fluffy clouds
Leave them trailing in our wake
Keep our path as we go
No room for mistakes
Onwards to our destination
Where we want to go
Our baggage in tow
And get there and go
Walk on to our next venture
Unwrap the bow
Let it all go
And enjoy our journey
We got there when we flew
Just us two
Out with the old
And in with the new
And onwards we go
Just us two

DAZE

My mind is a daze
Stuck in a haze
Hit like a whirlwind
Twisted like a gherkin
Wondering and staring
Visually impairing
Hit by a truck
Caught in a whirlpool
Weird and wonderful
Beautiful and colourful
See you think this sounds bad
You think I am mad
But you will never understand
You will never see
The doors and their frames
Playing the game
Enticing me in
Whispering in the wind
Slamming in front of me
Crushing my dreams

And when they are wedged open
Mechanisms broken
I put my foot in
Out on a limb
What is on the other side
Is it a dark side
Or is it lit up
A light or a spark
Then you will see
What has become of me
Where I am at
Would you look at that
Would you see what I want you to see
Is it about you and me
No matter where I go
Wandering in the snow
Battling the rain

From the highest plain
No matter what the pain
There is precious love to gain
Weird and wonderful
Beautiful and colourful
Then you will see
What has become of me

Banish my thoughts
Start afresh
Put me to the test
Give me time to invest
Let me confront these demons
Whispering in my ear
I am writing for you
It is all I want to do
I battle against the page
Fighting through every line
Testing my skills
Words come at will
Every time I stop and think
Looking for the missing link
I think of you and me
And this is what I see

We have opened a door
Walked down a path
Crossed a bridge
Jumped off a cliff
Beat round the bush
Ran across the road
Floated in the breeze
With total ease
Dodged all of the raindrops
Wrapped in each other's arms
Twisted like the vine
Infused as one
Looking at your beauty
I had an epiphany
A message from you and me

And I saw what you see
Emotions slightly frayed
Lost in the haze
Feeling the intensity
Fractures in you and me
But you are not about to give up
Give up on me and us
Look at how far we have come
What we have done
Smiling beneath the sun
Look at what we have won
Working as one
Dreaming of what we have become
Looking back and sighing
At how quick it has come

But the time is now
To make our vow
Because the fork in the road
Has come up close
Up the road we go
Our whole life in tow
Holding your hand
Because I can
Safely on the other side
Wrapped in my hand
I have your heart
Beating so gently
I watch you with mine
So elegant and thoughtful
Considering and kind
Smiling and shining
You have me in your hand
I am part of your plan
To wander this world
Watching life unfurl
Sharing our experiences
Hugging and kissing
Talking and laughing
Dreaming and singing

Twinkling beneath the stars
Watching the world rotating past
Rising from the shadows
So warm from head to toe
Melting each other's hearts
Now knowing where to start

Start from above
Like the soaring dove
This is the reality
What has become of me
What do you believe
After what do you see
Weird and wonderful
Beautiful and colourful
Where I am at
Sitting in this flat
Thinking and dreaming
Silently breathing
The next installment due soon
I can already feel it
Working through my mind
Soon it will be time
And as long as you are mine
We will be fine

ONE

Sometimes I feel crazy
Thoughts whirling around in my head
I sit here and think
Like I'm writing in ink
On a bloodstone I call my heart
I paint a picture
Like a work of art
About what I was
Right from the start
Loving
Living
Kind as you are
Looking at life
Like I was living afar

Different I was
The weird boy at school
I believed in it so much
That I embraced the name
It became my tag
As sad as it was
And I carried on with my life
But coming off worse
I only dreamed of love
It was my ambition
Addiction
Of choice

As sad as it seems
I never believed
I would find the one
And in all that I found
It was never the one
Voices in my head
Driving me on instead
Swishing and swirling
Sloshing around
Alarm bells ringing

I'm out of town
I'm out of there
And somewhere else
And I am not going back
It's this way or else
So on I go
Marching on
To the next adventure
Or the next failure
And family and life
Love and concern
These were the things
That dominated what I earnt
What I made of myself
What I became
Always overshadowed
Always in pain

Everything else
And everyone
Did what they did
For number one
And understandably so
As they all dropped away
I was the only one that stayed
But I had no play
No tactics
No rhythm
Just circling around
Like a spinning top
And it didn't stop
It kept on going

Reading like oak
Layers of past
And layers of future
Rings on a stump
Tree of life
Branching out
All I wanted to do

Was stomp and shout
My mind was a whirlwind
I couldn't catch a breath
And so, defense kicked in
My immune system grew
As the mode wore on
My personality wore on
Wore down or worn up
It didn't matter
My heart was a mess
Served on a platter
I knew I was done
Alone in the field
Fruitless
Tasteless
All worn out
No ray of sunshine
Or beautiful sunset
No chirping in the distance
Just instant regret
Remorse
Or dread
Hunt or be hunted
My best challenge yet

Grow strong
Lead
Service your people
Become who they need
But keep at a distance
Further away
But never too far
Always enough
A half full jar
Everything sectioned
Organized
Shaped
Everything on order
No great shakes
No issues

No worries
Everything tied up
Wrapped and packaged
Safe and protected
Pandoras box
Open or not
No can for me
The worms can rot

I will blossom
Burst open with awe
Become the shining light
They cannot ignore
Be needed
Wanted
Get everything right
That is the job
Of any shining light
So, I left the field
In search of my glory
Found a small path
And went on my journey
And it felt good to get back
Up on my feet
Surge and move on
And skip to the beat
And I left my home
All of my comforts
And I went and found you
And never looked back
When you joined my path
It was all that I asked
To find my equal
To have the one

And so there you were
And my head was clear
I could finally think
Whilst standing right here
And as the world slowed down

And you were the one
The only one
Right there
In front and as one
One ray of light
Breaking the clouds
Streaming to the earth
Crossing your vision
Just beaming light
Full of energy
Warming the fields
With a streak and a shadow
And it is more than enough
To warm a heart
Radiate across
And reach out inside
That one ray of light
At that one moment in time
Letting me reach out
And knowing it will be mine

And with my mind now clear
I can inspire and think
And that is how
I write with ink
Blood on a stone
I bleed for you
Emanating my love
Straight back to you
And as I sit here
I sit back and think
How nice it is
To chill and think
About my life
And everything I have
Sometimes I think crazy
About everything I had
And have
And will have
With you by my side

My heart bursting out
And beaming with pride
And throughout this journey
Of thoughts running in my mind
I process the equation
That love is blind

Blind as a bat
With no expectation
Limitless surprises
Challenges to be won
Prizes are priceless
Wonders are awe
All of our days
Never lived before
Creating history
Endless story
Legacies
Energies
Never ending fun
Whenever the fuss
The stress and the stuff
I journey my circumstances
My learnings and us
And everything in between
And onward it seems
Because it never stops driving forward
The voices in my head
Screaming at me instead
Telling me my future
Making my bed

So I'm lying in it
Loving it
Counting it down every day
I am to the right
And you to the left
And every time I turn
I get you instead
Of nothing

No one
I get the one
That's what I won
Your what I'm winning
And I'm your prize too
It is just us two
Everyone outside
Give us the room
It's our time now
So give us the room
To blossom
And wander
Drifting across the plain
Hearts melted to happiness
Our love ingrained
Intertwined
Wrapped up as one
And our minds and our thoughts
Ever as one

RHYMES AND RHYTHMS

I kick back and relax
Think of the past
Thinking away
Wandering away
Thoughts and feelings
Games and their dealings
Chipping away
Going away
Coming back
With a roar
Greetings galore

New people and faces
Watches and traces
Watching the clock
For the next tick and tock

Making decisions
Whispering derisions
Folding and baulking
Pondering and prospering

Wishing for dreams
Trying to believe
And wondering and waiting
Awaiting the faith
Staying awake
And realizing that this could be
The only truth for me

Life packs no punches
Moral indignity
Of what it does
To you and me

Life is oblivious
Facts and figures
Calculations
Connotations
Speculations

We make our own luck
To prevent being stuck
Caught on the precipice
Stagnant and lonely
Awaiting the date
Of the endless faith
That life will show you
To guide you
Inspire you

But the truth today
Is that you make your own way
Escape the clutches
Of your heartless emotions
Listen to the true ones
The delicate and quiet ones
Announce them promptly
To your mind and soul
Watch as it points you
Towards your goal

The answer will find you
When your mind brings it to light
And then you will find
Long awaited respite
Because you will find it
Sometimes you will expect it
And sometimes you won't
But you will get it

Then harness and protect it
Because it will bring you through
To what is true
Know that you want it
Believe it and own it
Always apply the rule

Go back to school
Learn your paces
Watch and learn
Search and earn
Always yearn

For the next best thing
The benefit it will bring
Don't let it sting
When you miss your turn
Just step back and correct it
Move on strong and stern

Make of me what you will
But truth holds still
Hangs in the air
Will you just stare
Or reach out and grasp it

As for love let it find you
Because that it will
Release you from the ties
The rain as it cries

Unwrap the wrapper
Strip it down
Look and frown
Turn it around
And fold it in two
Then it becomes new

The two of you
Only one way to go
Never leaving our eyes
Following the sky
Watching the clouds drift
Staying on course
For the peace we source

I will always be there
Waiting for you
Watching the fortress
Protecting our boundaries
Keeping the clause
The shroud and the bond
As I wrap back the wrapper

Yet only light surrounds us
Because no matter the choice
The decision you make
Nothing else matters
Not the world that shrouds us
Just me and you
I will always hold true

When the sun turns blue
Will I consider leaving you
Now calculate the chances
And see where it gets you
I smile at those words
The irony of it all
Standing so tall

Whilst we scratch beneath the surface
So elegantly and effortlessly
You become inspiration

Whilst all else is worthless
Whatever you do
Between me and you
Only you shine
Like a rhythm and rhyme
For all of time
You will be mine
I will be yours
That's all there is to say
Now enough for today

BLUE TOUCH PAPER

I'm here
I'm there
Here and everywhere
My conscience
Is on to it
A dare will no longer scare
Whatever approaches me
Whatever storm might come
I am the one
The mighty one
The only one that can change
Adapt and extract
The info that I need
Redeem it
I own it
Never will I fear
I've taken the knocks
They have dropped me down
Spat at me
Kicked at me
Heightened all my fears
Life blew up on me
Struck at me
Annoyed me
Controlled me
It owned me
Exposed me
Destroyed my frontier
My fortress
Was in distress
I had to address
The mess that was eating me alive
Stripping my skin
All pouring in
The haters
Excuse makers
The worst in the pile
Devoured me

Choked me
Destroyed it all
They made me become
A zombie
Lifeless
All washed out
Dead
Pulse stopped
On the deck
Life support
Was needed
To save me
Awaken me
Lighten up my life
Beep beep
The sound of a beep
The quiet
The open
The whisper of the wind
The only thing in sight
Well it is not
It is invisible
Just responsible
For fooling you
For the sound
Is invisible
The only thing
That is really true
Is the anticipation
The expectation
The hope
The faint hope
The silent prayer
The vision
The rhythm
Of the heart
To start
The only thing
That will get the mark
To save me

The savior
The blue touch paper
Lightened up
With the spark
Now making the mark
Blow up in smoke
Start to choke
Start
Light Up
Please please beat
And those voices
Faint voices
Those are what I heard
I listened
Envisioned
Strained to reach out for the light
I came back
Jumped on the track
And started running
Believe it I was running
To reach its glory
Feel it's warmth on me
Start all over again
Reach out through my pen
And own the rest
Live up to the test
And pass it
Smash it
Forget about it
Move on
So that's what I do
Between me and you
Never better
To the letter
Or the book
Whatever
It's there
I got it back
My mojo is back
It smacks of innocence

A godliness
A holiness
But it's there
Up in the air
Unleashed
Strengthened
Mighty all over again
And it's different
It's stronger
I will own it for longer
The hunger
Desire
The endless games
But power through
Is what I will do
Because that's what I want
The only thing I want
Apart from survival
Is knowing what I know is true
The only thing that keeps me here
Is knowing I've got you
Honestly
No word of a joke
I will openly revoke
All claims against that rhyme
Because the only truth
Is in those lines
Stood the test of time
The females in our lives
As men
Repent
Take everything back you said
Just respect
And listen
To the only thing that's true
Can't live with them
Can't live without them
Like I can't without a pen
To write these things
A woman in my life

The only thing that's right
Same for you
You know it's true
That is your safety
Through and through
Whatever my story
Or the lessons from yours
Or theirs
Them him or her
We have all been through
The darkest of days
I can only say
That it was yesterday
So there we all leave it
Because unless you can prove otherwise
Physics prove otherwise
That you can't go back
Or bring it forward
You and me can only let go
In time
It heals
The open wound itself
The one I thought
The last one of all
That had finished me off
Gone for good
Well and truly
All over
Yet I'm writing this rhyme
For all time
It will be there
Forever in the future
It stays
Don't go away
There is plenty more to come
To share with you
So never will we be through
Or in the past
We will be
But for present and future just see

Just you watch
Spin the clock
In hundreds of years we won't be there
But a hundred years ago
We weren't there either
Just here
In this moment
This is where we own it
And make the most of it
That is the bit
That makes everything alright
Sit tight
In person
In spirit
Or on the ride
White knuckle
Here we come
Churn me up inside
Let's go
Down low
Right up
Side to side
What a ride
With more to come
Whisper it quietly
We are just as one
Boom
Bang
Whoop there it is
As I lean unto you
I would be remiss
To not give you a kiss
And a hug
And a lover
And a whole lot of other
I am but a lot of things
But only in love with you
Stands true
Holds up
Unstuck

I only belong to you
In the present
And the ever-drawing future
Metaphorically
On every sketch
I will etch
A picture of me and you
Us
Forever
And ever
The end

CHAPTER FIVE

WHEN ALL IS LOST

This time it was 'true love' that came, saw and conquered. I was at the top of the mountain of life. Surely, I had never been so happy before? Of course, my previous experience was still love, but the love experienced by a boy and a man is quite different. This was the type of love that you read about in novels and watch in the movies – this woman was 'the one'. I thought I was meant to spend the rest of my life with my 'forever girl'. When it ended, I landed with a thud that reverberated across every aspect of my life. It was a tragedy that I did not foresee. I went into my thirties now tangled in an even denser web of emotion than ever before. But this time I knew with the benefit of hindsight that each strand had to be hand picked apart in its own unique way. I had become more reflective and therefore more positive and resilient. My psychology was changing, and I owed it to myself to dig deeper than ever to understand what happened.

These 13 poems express my journey into *self-reflection*:

1. WORDS OF A STREAM
2. WHERE DO I GO
3. END OF THE LINE
4. THE TIME HAS COME
5. GOODBYE
6. ALWAYS BE THERE
7. FOREVER GIRL
8. MOVE ON
9. ONE DOOR CLOSES
10. THERE WILL ALWAYS BE LIGHT
11. FUTURE
12. GLISTENING WITH HOPE
13. ENCORE

WORDS OF A STREAM

We argue
We fight
Try to put things right
We shout
We scream
Because we dare to dream
We chase perfection
Live with complexion
We suffer the pressure
Of endless expectation

But it is right
We are both right
With everything we say
We care
Compare
In the light of day

The sun is shining
The birds are in song
We do all we can
Just to get along
And we do
With time
Put everything right
The delight
Not quite
But we do stay tight
Because we are
Who we are

Both me and you
Two separate people
Working as one
It's nature
Human
To want what we want
To like what we like

To always be right
I've wrote about acceptance
Once before
Never so true
With feelings galore
I know we can do better
Better than before
Keep learning the learnings
And dream ever more

We never leave
Or walk away
Because we rise to the occasion
Day after day
We wake up and own it
Work harder than before
Learn and grow
Forever more
Go to work
Or just walk to the shops
Loving the feeling
Steaming so hot
Under the collar
Rising up the spine
Hairs on end
Knowing you are mine

And in time
Everything heals
Dust settles
Hot from our heels
As we race
Chase
Move from last base
Keep running
Yearning
To get to our goal

Get there we will
Top of the hill
At the precipice
Never stand still
Keep rising
Constantly yearning
Dreaming
Searching
Soaring to the top

We are on top
Despite the arguing
Growing and learning
From every last fight
My heart screams
Yours burns
What can we gain
What can we learn

Learn to stay positive
To keep strong
Because in each other's arms
Is where we belong
On song
Right on cue
Back again
Just me and you
I wrote it
For you
I write this
For you
Just us two
All there is
Just us two

An endless bliss
Or abyss
Cycle
Circle around

We constantly show
What we are about
And what you show
What you mean
In your endless cycle
A true love stream

Flows
And goes
Onwards it goes
The waves
The current
Never strays
Soaks up the rays
Of the sun every day

It ripples
And ruptures
And takes many hits
From humans
And nature
That bends it out of shape

And the feeling
It grates
That perfection is wavered
As it hustles
And bustles
And froths at the sides
It swishes
And sloshes
And sprays all around
But carries on
Goes on forward
Carrying weight around

But remember the river
Is on the shoulders of earth
On the precipice
The top
Of earth all around
The river
Your feelings
They are quite the same
Bear life
House life
And emanate all around

They protect life
Give life
And constantly go
And despite the torrents
And abject failure
And disaster
Catastrophe
Onwards they go
They flow
And whisper
And shout
All about
Always there
Through every scare
Always they go
On

Turn it on
Watch it and wonder
It outlasts us
Watches over us
And gives us our smiles
We look out to water
I mean I meant sea
Wander the coastline
Stare at the horizon
Mind blowing
Craziness

Awe at its vastness
Never defeated
Bellowing out waves
It calms us
Looks after us
Feeds us
Feeds life
Feeds the sun
The atmosphere
The stratosphere

Everything we have
Our life
Our life
Everything we have

Sun gets the credit
For us being alive
The plants
Oxygen
Or even the wind
But water recycles
And endless cycle
Of life
When it emerged
Billions of years ago
It came from the sea
Like just you and me

Don't you see
How they both compare
You
Your feelings
The ocean
It's beginnings
The rivers
It makes
Wrapping around the earth
Like you
All around me

Consume me
You do
You protect me
Affect me
And help me breathe

You warm me
Comfort me
Help me survive
You care
You share
You make me care
You make me wonder
Admire
Inspire
You make me smile
For a while
Ever more

Your there all the time
Always there
You share with me
All you can bare
That's cheeky
I know
But I know you so
You will rupture
In laughter
And circle around
Like a drop
In the lake
Your love dissipates
In circles
Repeating
Spreading around

It rings
Sings
Vibrates in the light
Runs on forever

Try as I might
I count
The rings
And constantly try
To follow those things
To the end
Till the end is nigh
But onwards they go
Never do they show
Weakness
That affects this
Because that's not on show
What we are watching
In all our wonder
Is water
And thoughts
Of how amazing it is
How it is always there
Ready to share
Ready to own
Your point of view
That's what it is
That's what I mean
That's the moment
Of an endless love stream

And when we fight
Remember that thought
That picture
That time
When you stood as mine
In wonder
From your slumber
Remember these words
When you feel bad
Or feel sad
Remember these words
These thoughts
These pictures
They are both the same

A stream
And you
And all there is to gain
All there is to feel
And appreciate
The deal
That's what it is
This is what it is

Wonderful
Amazing
That I am with you
And you with me
Like looking out to sea
All that we want
All that we can be
There it is
That's what I'm talking about
You have cracked smile
And so, have we
Me
And my soul
Have done the same
We are best friends
We are the same
We compare
We do that
We argue
We fight
But we are still the same

Have it common
Make a laugh
A smile
A flutter
A stutter
A murmur
A tremor
A feeling
A skip

Of a beat
Of me and you connecting
Sparking
Trespassing
Into the unknown
The excitement
The fright
The night
The feeling
Of being alone
In our bubble
That ripples with the waves

When we first met we were floating
Wandering into space
We soared
We did
In our own world we did
Heaven sent
Not hell bent
We raced to the stars
And looked back to earth
Imagined our luck
Of our paths crossing

We watched from space
And remembered how lucky we were
But now imagine
The forks of water
From every vision
How blue dominates earth
And that's where we came from
That's where our world
Drifted out
Through the streams

And then we got up and walked
On land and journeyed
Then crossed paths
Then found you
From ashes
And smoke
Oh how we soared
We spread out
Stretched our wings
And created this cycle
Of endless things

Before we flew
And drifted away
We had once drifted
In a different way
So now we can predict the future
Of what we may do
Let's get on with living
Just like we should do
Let's enjoy this first
Make these moments
This is the verse
That we will write about one day
Today
Tomorrow
Or whenever we do
Today is the day
That we will do
What it takes
What we will do
Is focus on us

Just me and you
That line
Just me and you
The perfect line
The perfect rhyme
To describe me and you
So here I will end it

This story of us
I'm signing off now
Because my work here is done
I was thinking of us fighting
And now I am rhyming
Of us
And us
Doing us
And being us

And what it means
True love stream
Ocean
Earth
Space
Stars
All words I have used
Sun
Light
Shining bright
All these words
Come from thinking of you

Isn't it amazing
Isn't it wonderful
For it to become this
On this day of all days
But become it has
Yes it did
And I'm thinking of you
And everything we have
And I'm happy
Not sad
Because that fight just reminded me
Of everything we have
And made me happy

So let's not be sloppy
Let's grow
And show
How we do things
And be proud
And keep going
Forever knowing
How great we are
Remember the words
Remember the moments
The pictures
The visions
Envision
The reason
Why we are still here

Don't fear
Don't despair
We will always be
A fragment right there
A bubble
No trouble
Just stand right there
And admire
Inspire
And wonder and hope
A true word we spoke
So wonderful
Bespoke
In all that we feel
This is what we wrote
These are our words
That keep us afloat

Surviving
Surmising
Wondering
Inspiring
Amazing

How good it all seems
And actually is
Amazing
Things
What we have
What we give
What we want
Can bring this response

So as I now go
I will leave this hanging
Just this one last one thing
This joy that you bring
With you
Is you
It is you being you

So after we have thought of all the good stuff
Let's focus on you
And focus we will
While you focus on me
And keep the circle
Flowing around

So remember that
And me
And see
What that does
Because that is great
Just as good
As us
So it is
That feels good too
Thank you
You just made me think
Of another ending
Because I can't keep writing
Or it will be never ending

So let's just say
We are great
No scrap that
We are better
Better than that
We are amazing
Flowing
Living the dream
Constantly flowing
Like words in a stream

WHERE DO I GO

How am I feeling
I just don't know
It doesn't feel right
I'm not in a flow
Words don't come to me
I just don't know
How do I pull through
Where do I go
So, it is what it is
My life is apart
Where did it all go wrong
How did the end start
Is it any wonder
I can't seem to contain
Is it any wonder
I'm in so much pain
I don't know where it started
I just know it is gone
Now all I know
Is I don't know where I belong
The end came
While I was still sleeping
Now it is over
And I am still sleeping
Dreaming
Walking
But always in night
How did I get here
How is this right
How am I feeling
I just don't know
It doesn't feel right
I'm not in a flow
Words don't come to me
I just don't know
How do I pull through
Where do I go
What is next

Give me a right turn
Left one
Or forwards
Give me a sign
Because right now
I'm in reverse
Going down a landslide
It is just getting worse
Heading backwards
Sliding in a daze
My whole life is on hold
Like seeing through haze
A whole new world
But it is all cold
Everything is blurry
Darkness all around
Whoever is there
Silence is my sound
The rest all echoes
Can't make it out
I'm trying to figure
How to work it out
Every day
I try to navigate
But I only end up
Back at square one
From the moment I wake
To the moment I sleep
I feel so lonely
I feel so meek
Wrapped up in my thoughts
That empty abyss
My whole life exists
To not exist
How am I feeling
I just don't know
It doesn't feel right
I'm not in a flow
Words don't come to me
I just don't know

How do I pull through
Where do I go
So does it start now
A bright new beginning
Spring turns to summer
All is forgiving
Birds tweet
Bells chime
The sun beats down
Over all time
And the world feels brighter
A whole lot nicer
The shadows whisper
Love lies in the air
Hope is strengthening
Everything feels like a win
All worth living
Living from within
But snap
There it goes
Clap
And it's gone
For right or wrong
So let me tell you
This whole new beginning
I'm done with its bidding
I've given my all
Yet I'm still lying on the floor
Down and out
Totally KO'd
All that hope
Was never worth having
A puff of smoke
And now it is all gone
So there it is again
It's all gone wrong
This song is not hope
For that is no more
This song is despair
For that I am sure

166

How am I feeling
I just don't know
It doesn't feel right
I'm not in a flow
Words don't come to me
I just don't know
How do I pull through
Where do I go
My final words
Are that the end is not nigh
Nothing good
Can come of this
Been there before
I have plenty of experience
Like I said
It is just empty abyss
So all there is
Is just me
Everything else
I can no longer see
However long
I just don't know
How long to endure
How low can I go
Will I shake it off
I just don't know
I've done it before
Such a long time ago
Last time hope came
And I lived the dream
Love was fluid
Flowing like a stream
Racing down river
I never thought it would end
No mind given to the ocean
On which everything would depend
We were at mercy to mercy
It was never going to happen
And so back to square one
Was always the outcome

I refused to believe
Remained defiant
I needed to be
A fearful giant
Shrug off any doubts
Build a legacy
Remember the hope
Feeds off its energy
But then
Smoke
The result is nope
Nada
Nothing
So now I am broke
Broken
The end
Game over
Again
Over and out
The usual trend
So let me be
As I need to be
I know the drill
I've paid the fee
Gained entry to empty
And now I am alone
Let me wonder
This timeless zone
Maybe I will
Or maybe I won't
I know if I don't
It will never be over
The only thing
Is what I always know
Don't let them come out
Never let them show
Hide the feelings
Protect inside
Seal off
Close the gates

And maintain the fort
So I shut down
Camp it out
Here for the long haul
Embrace the drought
No need to worry
I will go through the motions
Just without obvious emotion
Until I know it's right
If it does come
It will be the one
Then and only then
Will I see the sun again
So what is this for
What is the reason
I have to describe it
Before someone prescribes it
Labels my being
Not land of the living
But soulless
Not fit
For human companion
So I just don't believe it
If I cannot see it
Touch it or hear it
I guess it just is
So ask me
Go ahead
So how am I feeling
Because I just don't know
Nothing feels right
I'm not in a flow
Words don't come to me
I just don't know
How do I pull through
Where do I go
All I know
I can't see me
I'm lost
Hopeless

Helpless inside
Can't seem to stop off
Vacate the ride
On it goes
Whilst I'm barely surviving
And so it ends
With imperfect timing
Endless cycle
In a perfect circle
And if you are out there
Please set me free
And if you can't do that
Then please leave me be
This thing is over
All out at sea
This moment is over
There is nothing left of me

END OF THE LINE

I guess I just don't know
How I feel
You're tearing at my heart
I know you're not far away
We are never far apart
But I just don't know
If it is enough
If I should just
Give up

I want you close
I miss your smile
I want you near
Not a distant mile
I can't bear the thought
Another man you letting in
You were mine
Always have been

My patience is wearing thin
I want you back
Despite the fact
You stabbed my back
Broke my heart
It wasn't cool
Wasn't smart

My head is hurting
From all of this searching
For reasons it went wrong
This isn't a song
It isn't a rhyme
It is the only time
That you are truly mine

I'm talking to you
Screaming at you
Letting it all out
These words I write
Try as I might
Just keep letting you in

I was supposed to type
About my dilemma
My issue
Moment
Crossroads looming on
But as soon as I focus
On my purpose
The clouds come storming in
You take over
Now my life is over
Because I'm never going to win

This constant battle
Such a shambles
Always drawing me in
What does it do
Look what it becomes
Selling my soul to you
It bleeds
Weeps
Crushed and buried
I dreamt of a family
Of us being married

But now it is scattered
Thrown into the wind
Our time is over
For all that I've seen

I'm not saying I didn't hurt you
Or cause you pain
I know what I did
I feel ashamed

I am so very sorry
A thousand times
I can't take it back
Or do it again
I see you
There is hope
The lump begins to choke
My throat
My lungs
Leading to my heart
I feel you
Sense you
Dare to dream again
Then you leave
And over it seems
And it's back to me with a pen

So I just sit here
A lonely figure
Cutting into the scene
But not all is as it seems
Shall I move on
Or stay right here
Go back to the path
Walk with no fear

Feel the stones crunching
Sun burning
Plough on forward
For it is all I have
Or stay here in sadness
Driving me to madness

Go it alone
Or carry the slack
I wanted you here
I wanted you back

So the moment has passed
And the silence is deafening
Looks like that's it
I'm on my own
Stand up
Be counted
But never be doubted
A time of my life
Never forgot

Forever remembered
No regrets
And so I lift my head
Lost in the scene
It's time to move on
My curious keen
Thanks for reading
My thoughts at the time
This is the moment
The end of the line

THE TIME HAS COME

The hardest thing
I've ever had to do
Is tell the one
We are no longer two
Our time has come
To a natural end
The dream is over
It won't come again
I looked into your eyes
To tell you the truth
My heart has left you
And I'm feeling scarred
Not that I've hurt you
For we both agreed
The time has come
To set ourselves free
To acknowledge our future
Is now a distant past
To know what we had
Has disappeared fast
It has faded to black
And gone with the wind
It is not coming back
We know we can't win
We have had our chances
Where we have dared to dream
Moments to cherish
Where we were both keen
But whatever was said
It never happened
You tried something new
You made my heart blacken
I still forgave you
My feelings had softened
I wrestled with notions
And I hadn't forgotten
What we had
It was all so special

But now it's gone
We vacated our vessel
And I hoped and longed
I pined for your love
To recover and move
To come back from the cusp
It has taken so long
For me to be done
We can't give anymore
We have done enough
The pinnacle
Glory
Of doing anything for you
The desire and hope
In everything I saw in you
When I think of these things
It hurts me to realize
That all and us
We are now through
I harp back to the past
Thoughts racing fast
Gleaming
Beaming
The memories vast
But being with you again
It could never last
The challenges we'd face
As rigid as cast
The doubts would resurface
Decisions would come
Quickly we would realize
What we would become
We would always love
And never run
But we were always doomed
The day would come
We could never be strong
Or stick to our guns
For our families around us
Would never be one

We would find this out
And soon would be done
Because in our happiness
The darkness would come
There could only be sadness
Destined to come
The forces between us
Would never repent
The fighting is endless
Battle-worn but relentless
It would always haunt us
And never diminish
Never let go
Fail to finish
Our connection and spark
Could never disguise
The fact of our situation
We can only surmise
Conclude that we can't
Change if we wanted
Trapped in a moment
Everyone around us created
We would always be happy
In times alone
But the consequences of that
Would always be thrown
Flying around
Affecting our lives
The fact that we could never
Just feel alive
Looking over
Our broad shoulders
Running from truth
And everything around us
We can't change it
Work or manipulate it
It will always be
The same as it is
Today
And yesterday

And every other day
The consequence of faith
Always having a say
I can only respect
The life that you've had
Only hope
In the life you could have
Yes, it is tragic
Of course, it is harsh
But you cannot deny
It would always be tough
Concessions to be made
Sacrifices in vain
Forever looking
For that runaway train
Unless we got away
Never planned to stay
Always moved
Running from truth
It could never work
And the reason why
Is that they will not change
We would live a lie
They will not change
They would rather it die
We can reason
Accommodate
Enjoy every date
Live for the moment
Try to anticipate
Predict and conclude
Let love exude
But the fact and the truth
Is that would only excuse
The fact that they
Could never understand
The fact that they
Would always stray
Stray from our path
And plan our every move

Our journey processed
Their acceptance a ruse
Because once we accommodate
The moment we negotiate
Our leverage is lost
Our honour forgot
And whilst I accept
That you should never give up
The respect would be lost
Because they would never trust
If they did
Their words would be different
Actions would show
A different component
Show a feature
A new element
One we could trust
One we could implement
But we can't
Because they don't
And it is what it is
And as harsh as it sounds
It is what it is
We lived in a bubble
Experienced a freak
We broke the mould
We set out to eat
Our cake
And we did
And it tasted good
We lived a high life
Just as we should
But I guess I always
I always knew
That the time would come
When we would be through
I can't deny
My emotions ran high
I told myself off
I wondered why

And as I pondered
I realized that
I couldn't fight it
Or take you back
I will always look back
On how you touched me
You showed my soul
Everything that I could be
You made me better
You made me a man
I know it sounds corny
But I was the man
My back was up straight
A spring in my step
I thought I had made it
A thought I had kept
I held it
Harnessed it
And became so much better
I learnt it
Grabbed it
Became a go getter
I owned it
Became a challenger
Clambered to the top
Loved by the letter
Committed forever
To you by my side
You changed the story
You turned the tide
So as I write this
With a tear in my eye
I know I have to
Whisper goodbye
I must move on
And embrace the future
Deny our past
From making me a loser
I cannot already allow
My hope to stall

Inspiration to wane
My tower to fall
I must admit
And own up to myself
That you've left a mark
In time itself
You will always be
A huge thing to me
No matter the story
You will never break free
You're a part of me now
A crease on my brow
A beat of my heart
A foot on the ground
A lasting impression
Of how love should be
A timeless masterpiece
A lock with no key
You meant the most
And always will
You will always be part of me
I will forever hold you still
But I have to focus
On what I can feel
On what I can see
And what I can do
Look to the future
Not what I came through
And when I think
I know I must find
The key to unlocking
The next move in my mind
What I describe
These thoughts in my mind
I whisper them once
I whisper them twice
I sense it's hard
It's certainly not special
It's the hardest thing
I've ever had to do

The hardest thing
To let go of you
What I must give
For my mind to let go
Is to accept the truth
The answer is no
Our life is over
Thoughts no longer one
I'm going alone now
Our journey is now done
I'm no longer with you
And I thank you for everything
This life that you gave me
It was everything
You went on and saved me
But I must now break free
The time has come
For me to be me

GOODBYE

You ripped my heart out
Tore it to shreds
That was the moment
The moment I dread
When I had to stand
Up and free
No longer you
No longer me
Just me
Alone
Falling from my throne
You no longer by my side
I can no longer hear your voice
Your noise
Sound
Just having you around
Your smile
Smell
So sweet you could never tell
What would come
How
It all came about
You whispered
Then shout
Spun it all around
And now I'm dizzy
Someone save me
I got to get out of town
The axe fell
The tale lost
Our journey over
The dream long forgot
Over
Done
Nothing left to tell
Just time for me
To be about me
And carve it out for myself

And so I did
Didn't call it quits
Opened my mind
Unlocked the door
It all hit the floor
One by one
My soul left me
No longer at one
With you
I'm through
Over between me and you
And so it crashes
Rips and smashes
Laid out across the floor
No longer more
And so
With the cupboard empty
Skeletons rested
Time to be woken
Time to be tested
Did the tour
Of the lonely halls
Walked for miles
Echoing in mind
I whispered
Frowned
Then turned it all around
Stood up
Breathed
And let out a roar
And as I have
Life moves on
Waits till your comfortable
Then throws you a one
Opportunity
Chance
Moment to grasp
As it does
It beckons the choice
And so

I have
A choice to be made
A card to deal
Bet to be laid
Down
On the table
All out right there
So the gauntlet begins
To play out before me
Isn't it ironic
The moment life gives
To force you to choose
In the quest for bliss
This path or that
It doesn't matter
Life is mine
Served on a platter
So I will choose
I refused to back down
Something big
Is about to go down
Back in town
My soul rescued
The time has come
To test my resolve
My trust
Is a must
I must get that right
Learn to be open
Learn to do it again
I'm a little nervous
I cannot lie
But the time has come
To say goodbye
Goodbye my friend
My soul mate
My voice
The air I breathe
The one I rejoice
I'm here

Or there
Everywhere
But I'm here
No fear
The past will not die
It will stay
Ingrained
Etched in the mind
And the choice is now upon us
To separate in kind
All you have done
What has become
Goodbye my friend
Our new journey has begun

ALWAYS BE THERE

Make you happy
It's all I want to do
Give it all to you
Show you what I can do
But it is over
Too late
Never to be the same
It was all in vain
In vain
In vain

But here I still am
In the palm of your hand
Hanging off
Your every word
And I know
That it's hard
Because we are still apart

But you have to understand
The plan
My plan
It is all about you
Everything you do
All that I can do
To make you happy
Believe it or not
I care
Every day
I think of you

In many ways
Think about our pride
In every way
For what we achieved
All that we saw
Lived for
Dreamed of

Built
And chased
It wraps around my brain
I just cannot explain
What the next move is
What to do
Or how to handle it
Or where it leaves us
Who to blame
All I know
Is it will never come again

I'm the same as you
I want to be happy
And you to be too
See I know you are right
About lots of things
My heart and my pain
My emotions and sadness
See I don't cry
But I do feel
I may not show
But my sadness grows

It grows when I lose things
Or get things wrong
It grows when I see you
Looking forlorn
When you cry I cry
What you feel I feel
Was always the way
Despite what you say
The discord
The disconnect
Was always a thing
I worked my hardest
Tried to bring
Spirit

Honesty
To fix it I tried
I gave it everything
Fight and guile
Helped to build
Started to field
Solutions
Answers
Hope and dreams

But the disconnect
The way you feel
Your needs and wants
And all the desires
Was so much
So great
That my mind gave out
I needed to provide
I needed to feel

And with all the hurdles
That I had to surpass
The ones with you
Or on my own
I jumped them
Outran them
And was on top of the world
You were happy
So were we
Life had given us
All we needed to be
To be at the top
Enjoying fruit
Peaceful
Happy
And everything in between
But the last hurdle
It loomed over us
The final piece
Before we could be free

Free from the building
Free from the work
Free to roam
Anywhere on earth

For if we were bonded
Life was with us
In our hands
Our plan
With no one to challenge
Because our union
Meant our life
Our voice
Our choices
We were so close
Yet so far
When it all crashed
So far apart

The disconnect struck
And the earth parted
Our house lay in ruins
Our emotional chord parted
And so you gave out
Along with me
The love we once had
Just not meant to be
Yet all I want
Is for you to be happy
Despite the sorrow
Plaguing my heart

It bleeds
And burns
But I have to learn
To survive without you
Where life is concerned
You will move on

And try you must
I sincerely hope
That you can learn to trust
Find the one
Who does connect
Find the one
Who is better than my best

If you find it
I know I will be done
But I also know
That you are the one
So all I can do
Is pursue your happiness
All I can do
Is live through you
My loneliness
My hurt
My pain and sorrow
One day will ease
As I no longer follow

I will soon rise
A new dawn will come
I will not follow hurt
Or the past we came from
I will live for my dreams
I will get up and see
Hit the reset
And learn to be free

For all there is for me
Are things to do
Stories to tell
Adventures to find
Moments to capture

So the heart beats strong
And no matter my venture
Or my future
That comes
It will continue to fight
Prove the doubt wrong
Your happiness I long for
Never will that falter
My faith in you
Is still ever so strong
And in your heart
I will always belong

You may be gone
But in your happiness, I appear
I will always live on
And will always be near
Please don't forget me
Forever will I be here
If your ever unhappy
And you shed a tear
Pick up the phone
And I will be there

I want you to be happy
I shall say it again
Not enough can be said
I cannot pretend
Too much to type
So much to express
I have to show you
Desperate to impress
Please always remember
Again and again
Hope and faith
This is not the end

FOREVER GIRL

How could I let
The best thing I've ever had
Slip through my fingers
Well I know it wasn't meaningless
I knew its power
I always had hope
But never enough fire
Not at the end
Not for the fight
It was not in spite
It was not you
We both had a choice
And our own things to do
I can write this song
Poem or whatever
I could go on forever
About me and you
My forever girl
Anyone could tell
That we had it all

Having a ball
We strode through the years
Conquered our fears
Walked the walk
And never looked back
That's what we had
Exactly that
And I will fight for the right
To win that back
Don't get it twisted
There is work to do
A big question
We both need to answer
It is not about love
Or life ever after
It is a question of if
We have the will to dream

The trust
Blindness
Following into the light
The moment to
Meet line of sight
Let everything go
Melt down the walls
And give it a go
Join hands
Let it flow
Side by side
Intertwined in our glow

I want us to stir
To rise from the ashes
Soar to our moment
Our bubble in the wind
For I have had my time
My moment of madness
Lived through my crisis
And everything in between
Crushed and lonely
Abject failure
But always knowing
That you are my savior
My one
And only
My forever girl
How can you tell
That you are my world
Dumbstruck
Spellbound
Kneeling at your feet

Can you see
I follow you around
My spirit binding
Not making a sound
I'm there for you
Holding you

Sensing every touch
Warm for you
Hot for you
I want it all so much
You are my crown
The jewel in my vision
The sparkle in my eye
I don't even have to try
You are just there
In every slide
And my thoughts
They love it
Seeing you everywhere
They go into overdrive
Simply looking up to the sky
And as I'm looking
Gazing across the plain
Watching the wind
Wash over the picture
Brushing the trees
In a gentle breeze

The sky settled blue
A wispy white hew
With the odd cloud hovering
Silent as they are low
My mind drifts
Staring at the sky

I watch a ray
This is the plain of day
It pierces the sky
Burning through a cloud
Streaks down to the plain
Latches on to the ground

My eyes run down
The golden straight line
A warm ring of gold
On the tip of the grass

And I started to look up
To follow it back to the sky
I don't know why
I just glanced to the cloud
And there it was
The key to the picture
The golden globe
They call the sun

The crème dela crème
And the moment was one
As it burst onto my eyes
Only the shades to save them
The moment came
There you were again

I saw that sun
And I felt you there too
Like you were you
Just standing by my side
With our eyes transfixed
On the exact same setting
Our minds focused
Our hearts pounding
The shiver on my neck
The words I never said
And then I looked to my side
And realized I was alone

But I knew what I felt
We shared that moment
That one heartbeat of time
We joined as one

I promise you
As my heart draws that picture
That I will follow your life
At every juncture
I will be there

In friendship or not
To do my best
To tie us in knots
Your path
My path
My oath to you
I whisper
The words
That you know are true

You gaze at me
Lovingly
Take my hand
I gasp at you
Chest pounding true
Touching your skin
Like the ray of sunshine before
Like electric
Sparking
Powering my senses
I'm suddenly defenseless
Then a warm embrace
Feeling your taste
Your warmth
Body
Heart and soul
And now it is there
A story
To unfold

I know it is there
It wants to be told
Shall we do it
Go for it
Let it go
A question we know
Oh don't let it be no
I guess what I'm saying
Is whatever it is
We had a dream once

A story of a kiss
Never a miss
It burst like a butterfly
In that single moment
Our life lit up the sky
We spread our wings
And learnt to fly
Our life blossomed
As we walked on by
I wanted to kiss you
I really did
Maybe if we do
This dream will become bliss
For now
I must be content
With a blow away kiss
Hoping and praying
That you caught that kiss
That's just about enough
To keep me going just now
I'm still in your life
Damn
Wow

MOVE ON

It was you that was there
You that saved me
Believed in me
Owned me
Stopped and stared
You picked me up when I was down
I was fooling around
Like a clown
Crying out for help
And there you were
You gave it
Forgave it
Just let it be
You looked to me
With adoring eyes
You pleaded to me for love

How do I deny
How do I reject
Only when I reflect
That I realize what I have done
I think about it
Every day
In every way
It is hard to say
What do I say
When I have none
No words
Or verse
To shape
Or converse
It is sad
I know
But I don't know
I don't know why
I deny
But I know that I love you so
It shows

You know
How far
I go
To show you everything
To give you my all
Through it all
To give you my heart to hold
To never let go
Steady as you go
Trying not to harm it
Protect it you do
Proud of it
You nurture it
To make me a better man
To help me
Set me free
From this mental mind

Of curse
Of resistance
Of defense
Of regret
I get shot down
And come out fighting
Defending
Defending
Everything I am
No matter what
How little or small
Things affect me
And my heart redresses me
Shields me
Distorts me
Bends me all out of shape

And it is not you
That causes it
All the time
It is many things
Anything

That can set my episode
Programs me
Records me
Knows me
Gets to me
And I do my thing
And I am trying to win
To battle with it
Defeat it
Turn it to you and me
Harness our strength
Build on our energy
Fight the dark spirits
Let my heart rest
So it can turn to you
Focus on you
Beat to its own beat

And in that rhythm
Let it beat
And let it spin
Let it believe
In this true love thing
The quicker I turn it
The better I am
The less likely I am
To get confused
To defend on you
Lean on you
While I sort myself out
At random times
Because I never know
When I will feel down
And let it show
But I am getting better
Put it in a letter
There is one thing I promise you
I will get better
Defences don't matter
Because I believe in you

I want you
I love you
And I am not letting you go
Oh no
It is me and you, you know
So what do you say
Let's put it behind us
Move on to the next verse
After settling the score
We need some more
Always want more
Fresh challenges
Next steps
Next chapter
The better it gets

ONE DOOR CLOSES

One door closes
Yet another then opens
That's what they say
With emotions in motion
Feelings ring true
When disappointment strikes
They circle your heart
And dominate your mind
When you are ready
To close that chapter
You reach for that door
And slam it shut
The bang in your mind
Reverberates for ages
The vibrations like scars
So hard to forget
You wonder where
The next moment lies
The moment of change
The cutting of ties
The chance to sever
The cord that bonds you
To the hurt that you feel
That dominates all time
See it is the memories that steal
All the happiness from inside
The pain and anger
It rages around
It can often seem
Like all hope is lost
All out of hope
The good times forgot
The lowest of lows
A tunnel with no end
Running from nothing
No hope in sight
But a spirit
Broken

Can always be woken
Light can shine
Where darkness rules
For whilst you are breathing
Never stop believing
Your heart is still beating
Full steam ahead
You get one shot
To make it in life
One opportunity
To make it your own
When one door closes
Another opens
You put your foot there
And don't let it shut
Fix up
Look sharp
And play your part
For time waits for no one
And the days run fast
As the calendar ticks
There is a trick
A trick I can tell you about now
Play the game
Don't settle
For the hand you are dealt
Set your target
Make it heartfelt
Don't stop
Keep trying
Always fight
To achieve your goals
Plan with precision
Think it all out
Stop at nothing
Stomp and shout
I know it can hurt
And I would never downplay it
But open that door
And soar right through it

Smash through the barriers
Believe in your right
To realize your destiny
Don't think twice
Life is yours
No time to waste
You will make it though
You can win the race
One door closes
And others open
Don't walk through
And forever be broken

THERE WILL ALWAYS BE LIGHT

Things happen
How they do
The things they are
And what they do
My words for you
Will always ring true
The choices
We make
The many mistakes
We want it
And lose it
Just hope it comes right back
But relax
Sit back
Remember the drag

That small life moment
At the end of the smoke
That time
When you think
Wish you had ink
To jot down
As a reminder
The thoughts that play in your mind
Unwind
Let loose
Shake it all off
This is the part
Where we lift off
Gone with the wind
Forgetting our sins
Living the life
And freedom we desire
The empire
We build
Let it hold still
Cherish the moment
Always as one

Those times
We enjoy
The memories
We build
They are just but a fraction
Of everything we have
Our voices
Our connection
Our sadness
Our emotion
It tells me to say
We are full of devotion

Much travelled
Well experienced
Always together
With little interference
Small things
Try to get in
Big things
Explode
But our life holds still
Stands firm
Holds tall
And never shatters
Because none of it matters
We are who we are
Through a life of choices
The unknown plan
Rolling along

I always see cracks
We always see danger
But we live on
Hold on
And we don't let go
We won't
We can't
Would be terrible to believe
That we could

And go on
With things never the same
But they are
Right now
Within our grasp
We can
Lock it down
Sealed with a clasp
We can tap it
And stop it
Then harness it
Feed it
And watch it grow

With hope
Belief
And a sprinkling of freedom
It blossoms
And blooms
And one thing stays true
That love
In any form
Will always win over
This life
Of choices
And things
And moments
So when cracks grow
And chasms open
We will always face them
With eyes wide open
One true love
It is meant to be
So it is there
Laid bare
To see

My feelings in the open
I will always love you
Will always be hoping
I will be there
Through thickness and thin
My heart within
Racing to win
Your love
And companionship
And friendship
Or more
Whatever way
Shape or form
I will be here
To keep you warm
To hold you
Feel you
Wrap you up tight
For our true moment
To be shown in this life
We are in this together
There will always be light
It burns
So true
Forever and always
Will I truly love you

FUTURE

I'm not mad
But I cannot lie
My world has spun
Upside down
Oceans gone
Well run dry
This desolate wasteland
Is all I've got
And empty dreams
With all else forgot
All the hurt
The struggles
And pain
All that endured
All that in vain

I remember the good times
I feel them and squeeze them
For every last drop
Of all that love forgot
Because it is over now
Change has come
The dream of love
Thy kingdom come
Now just a dream
That chapter is done

I still can't believe
It has come to this
But I'm not mad at you
I'm just staring at the abyss
Because I am lost
Not found
The glory hasn't returned
The grass is not greener
Just lessons learned
It's harder
Bleaker

This outlook of mine
It's tougher
Harsher
Nothing intertwined
Just lonely
And cold
Like growing old
I'm weary
Dreary
No longer bold
I'm strong
I can fight
Work through the night
I'm getting on
Trying to move on
Kidding myself
That things are alright
And they are
On the bar
Sitting midstream
Or on the fence
Or whatever
Just ticking
Over

That is
What it is
Just ticking over
Nothing to look to
Nothing to inspire
Just desolate
Quiet
With no plan
Just going against the flow
Like facing a dam
And what shocks me
Stuns me
Amazes my brain
Are the feelings
That I'm feeling

It is driving me insane
But I'm feeling It
Pain
And sadness
And that
But also love
And happiness
And the things I once had
I yearn for them
Call out to them
Wishing them true
Just one more moment
One more chance
To be with you
The opportunity
Sensitivity
The chance to survive
Just one day
One hour
One minute
Whatever
Just the chance to feel it
One more time
To be with you again

Remember the time
When this sounded like madness
What happened to us
Where did we part
But then there they are
The questions
Thoughts
Wrapped up in my mind
And it just goes to show
My process
My affairs
Where I am at
I'm sad
But happy
Lonely

But peaceful
I look to the future
With no plan at all
I miss you
Could kiss you
Hug you and all
But I've accepted
Realized
That we can't have it all
We had love
True love on ecstasy
We lived the dream
Conquered with ease
Explored the world
Lived with riches
Grew our lives
With experiences and knowledge
We planted our souls
And built a life
We overcame
Hardship and strife
We built a house
And we celebrated our lives
We toasted to a future
Of endless surprise
And we fought for it
Bled for it
Gave it our all
And now we can look back
With wonder and awe
But as it is over
And I'm back in the room
Reality sets in
The dream goes boom
Or pops
Or whatever
The bubble has burst
There I go again
Dreaming of it all

So what comes first
Is a big dose of the truth
I recite what has happened
And start again
So now I build
To my new future
Spin my earth
Right back around
I will work on it
Grow it
Go forward
And on
The stage is set
Up I get
Up and away
And the story rolls on

GLISTENING WITH HOPE

So, after meeting
Leaving
Then living separate lives
We had a run
With another soul
We ended up making ties

Made our plans
Planted roots
Built foundations
Created life
Felt the good times
And the rough
Forgotten
We were
In each other's minds

A narrow memory
Lost in time
To be expected
As we lost contact
No fault of our own
We couldn't have known
Our initial contact
Was a whisper in the wind
But in that fleeting moment
Was where the tale begins

A tale of coincidence
In commons
And plenty of smiles
There is a tale of joy
Happiness
Curiosity
And talk of walking miles
Calories
Caramel
Party tunes galore

Who could have believed
We would hit the dance floor
Six years ago
Where it all began
Six days ago
And now we stand
Enlightened
Enhanced
Inspired by thought
Provoking words
Captivated and caught
We woke up this morning
In the aftermath of a whirlwind
After an evening of adventure
In which we were both glowing

Glistening with hope
Faith and desire
Swept from our feet
Our fire was ignited
Our passion was burning
How it happened
I'm still recollecting

I wanted you close
To feel your soul
I wanted to hold you
Be so bold
But whilst in our fervor
My mindset came
Nerves overtook me
My energy waned
I must tell you
For I must say
We did not lay
For all of our passion
But we did end up
Together in tandem

I wanted you so much
But not in this fashion
I wanted to lay with you
With so much compassion
In our fervent stupor
I felt not this component
And so, in turn
There was not that moment
I hope you will not feel
In anyway responsible
I hope you will not feel
Disappointed looking back

You are so beautiful
Inside and out
I am so complex
I have been throughout
My whole life
I have cherished contact
The moment to share
To be as one
I respect it so much
And I will hope for a reunion
To be sober and conscious
In a blessed union

It is burning my mind
But I pray that you are happy
When you say you are
I want to believe
That you will come back

I will be waiting here
My heart will be beating
To hold you near
To still be believing
I want a chance
To make you feel goose bumps
I want a chance
To make you hair stand on end

Stroke you
Kiss you
Service your grace
Feel your heartbeat
In passionate embrace
Giggle and whisper
Nibble on your ear
Feel out of body
And out of mind

It feels like eternity
Please join the race
Hurry back here
I can't wait to see your face
For I am missing you
Not a moment is too soon
To continue this tune

I could carry on writing
Forever more
In hope and longing
For you to walk back through that door
Have a good day
And please be safe
Keep on smiling
And never lose faith

ENCORE

So, this is it
How I feel
Not damn strait
Or an even keel

This is what I do
Make things complicated
Emotionally scared
Confidence eradicated

Whatever I do
I screw things up
Once or twice
But more than enough

And I'm used to how it feels
That's the worst thing
And I love who you are
That's the best thing

But alas what I do
Is make a fool
Off my perch
Fall from my stool

Then forever back
Comes back my emptiness
Quiet and peaceful
But deprived of happiness
Starved in fact

It is so damn obvious
I don't know what I'm doing
Or if it's relevant
I've strayed from course

Just taking wrong turns
It is all so unpredictable
Result inevitable

Sooner rather than later
I must end this slump
Before I end up with
Well you know what I mean

I aspire to think like you
So happy and free
To be who you are
See how you see

Like I could control these thoughts
Eating at my mind
But my resistance is futile
I feel so blind
From all of the fighting
This raging war
I need to escape
Before I'm no more

So that's all I'm saying
Is that I make it complicated
Until all is lost
As if it was fabricated

Soon I will lose it
You won't come back
Then I go back
To being alone

I hope I am wrong
And this doesn't come to pass
Don't get me wrong
I want it to last

I want to show you
Who I can be
What it is like
To be with me

My complex mind
Might be getting in the way
I don't know what to do about it
I don't know what to say

A feeble excuse
So low of a man
To think like this
In a way you can't stand

I get it though
Completely understand
Don't hold it against you
You deserve a better man

I will try
I can promise you that
To win this war
And end it like that

I hope the day
Will come to pass
When I truly let go
Of the distant past

The day when I
Will struggle to relive
All that has come
Way before this

When that day comes
I will know I'm free
To go on and live
How I want to be

I truly want that
I want that with you
Let's get real
That's how I feel

I don't know what
Will come of this
The so what's and the why's
What for's and what if's
Will be if you will
Will be what it is

Maybe I will get there
I want nothing more
Only time can tell
If there can be an encore

CHAPTER SIX

REBORN

Two years had swiftly passed, and I was rapidly approaching the path which led to this very book. I was reflecting, and for the first time in my life I let my mind rule my heart and I listened to my soul. My epic journey of 'love and heartbreak' had been a rollercoaster. My first heartbreak had a tragic air about it as I reached the darkest points of my boyhood life. The second, more intense heartbreak led to a whole new set of grown-up voices in my mind. All these years later and I was still in pain from these two experiences, but they had now become independent from me. I was able to detach from my emotions and write freely from a safe distance. There was a thick wall of immunity building deep within me and with that protection I was able to objectively consider these heartbreaks like a scientist observing an experiment; detached from the outcome yet eager to record the data. I had finally untangled myself from the demons that haunted me. This newfound freedom of expression was liberating. The voices had changed course; now they were seeking something different. It was no longer dark, no longer cloudy. I was becoming reborn.

These nine poems express my journey into *healing:*

1. FRIENDS
2. CHAOS
3. THE GAME
4. THE PEOPLE
5. QUESTIONS
6. WAKE UP
7. THE SYSTEM
8. MONEY
9. VOICES

FRIENDS

My friends
It depends
What do you want me to say
You trust in them
And ride with them
Climb the mountain
Raise the stakes
Confide
Reside
Take all you can take
You want to impress them
Show them what you got
That's your lot
And then it's not
The fear is literally too hot
The heat
The fire
Light up the spire

You take it
Ache for it
Burn for it you must
Because that's what it means
Total trust
All that it seems
Is that it's a must
A must have
A must want
All is forgiven
All is forgot

I'm there for you
Hurt for you
Give it all I will
Because I want you
Need you
And I can't stand it
My stomach is sick

But I can't be alone
I need to be accepted
Can't face it alone
Those wandering corridors
The neglect
Unnoticed
The things we all expect
Because without it we are lost

Journey through time
Whisper in the breeze
Forever in time
We lust for people
In our lives
People we trust
To serve us likewise
Acceptance
Rejection
It dents our pride
And everything else besides

A game of two halves
This world in our lives
Beat it we will
Or it will be our demise
Eat us alive
And spit us out
Life becomes a drought
No one about
Then you drift
Along the open plain
Anonymous again
Alone again

Journeying on your own
Monotone
Empty
Lifeless
Alone

But zip
Scrap that
Forget it ever was
Or is
Or will be
Because I still have a choice
For a distant future
One that suits me
One that wants me
The one that owns you
You know the one
Your future

The one you make
The steps you take
That's the one
The one you have
That's the one
That always has
Always having a ball
Enjoying the moments
That friends provide

Forgive
Forget
Or walk away
They are only choices
When friends come to play

CHAOS

This life
It's a mess
I beg to contest
This famine
This torture
This endless emptiness
I thought I was good
But there you are
To make me think
To make me start
You enrich me with happiness
Then wrench it away
You part with emotion
But keep me at bay
You need my attention
But in so many ways

Me at my best
Every single day
All the seconds
The moments
All of life's components
I offer to you
Give to you
I long for it
Crave it
Want it forever more
But it drives me crazy
Gets me anxious
Of what there is in store
You are my mind
And my mind is chaos
My heart rages war

With all that you say
What you do
And tell me
What you tell me to be
I always follow you
Forever letting you lead
But I wrestle
With these thoughts
They are burning within
I feel like I'm out there
In an endless whirlwind

Its caught me
Haunts me
It dominates my life
Don't do this
Don't do that
It's not true
That's a fact
Like sirens
Blaring
Always scaring
Keep this straight
Make this that
Oh when will it begin
To cease
Hold
Start to grow old
Be over
Leave me
Let me find my peace
Because if it isn't this
Or it isn't that
It's this
Or the other
Then I'm back to square one

People
Love
Life and its process
It's priceless
Limitless
In all that it will throw
At you
To trip you
Knock you off your path
Then love comes along
Makes you feel strong
Then that knocks you off too

And after all that
You're left with your mind
And you want it to be nice
You want it to be kind
But all that does
Is send you within
In endless hope
That something new begins
And as you search
Throw caution to the wind
You end up further
You begin to spin
Round and round
And round you go
Nothing left
You're in slow mo
Lost in your mind
Alone in your life
So it all catches up
And strikes you down
No more whirlwind
The drama has gone
The door is closed
To the world beyond

Now the voices
The soul of your mind
They all take over
Till they leave you blind
Before you know it
You're in the routine
You settle in moment
There's no in between
And as this goes on
You survey the scene
You even admit
It's all obscene
But there you are
Trundling along
If it were written
It's a somber song
Playing in the background
Whilst you repeat the tone
It follows you everywhere
Always alone

So everything is
Just how it is
Your moment of happiness
Your constant bliss
It's all you have
The thoughts in your mind
Things will happen
All throughout time
But above all else
You have your mind
This amazing nothingness
Commentating on your eyes
Making you breathe
Helping you feel
Keeping you straight
On even keel

You make your choices
Feel like your right
Fight for the previous times
When you've sparked it alight
Your body
For a second
You've found time to relax
Closed your mind
Sent it all back
Switched off the switch
And forgotten it all
For a very brief moment
It can all go away
Then boom
Bang
Back in the room
It all comes black
Flooding towards you

Moment passed
You're back in life
Whatever your poison
You know it was nice
But it cannot last
So you take back control
Next up is tomorrow
Who knows what it holds
But it's there
If you dare
A day of discovery
Another chance
For life to change
So I guess what I'm saying is
Just keep going
You just keep on
It keeps on coming
Everything in life
Is just endless chaos
You know what I'm saying
There is always something

So either
Sit back
And enjoy the ride
Or get up and go
And control the right
Fix the problems
Find the solutions
Then deal with your mind
And find absolution

Make a tidy home
For a tidy mind
Affairs in order
For a peaceful mind
Lack of stress
Is a happy mind
And lucky in love
The perfect mind
Smile and a kiss
A mind of bliss
Clean your mind
Go on like this
Not like me
It's not the best course
As chaos it is
It's what I've got
My only lot

So that's what I chose
Because I have to live
To live life like this
It's my humble abode
My design
My flaw
The hand I was dealt
I cannot complain
I can't change anymore
My mind is me
And I am my mind
Despite its failings

I must repay it in kind
I might be crazy
The war may rage on
But it's what I have
Where I've come from
So let chaos reign
For I choose to survive
To live this life
With my mind by my side

THE GAME

This life
Our affliction
Inhale it like addiction
Our distinction
Our reason
It sets us all apart

Different seasons
Lands and kingdoms
Association
Relations
Loyalty
Respect
It pulls us all apart

Strangers rule us
Whilst money blinds us
Beats us down
Controlled all around
Lifeless
Soulless
Conscience not making a sound

Love defines us
Our spirit and our souls
Our bodies and our minds
Benefit in kind
But our desires stretch us
Can drive us crazy
People like dominoes
Our hearts doing the rounds

We are superstitious
Suspicious
Ridiculous
At times
Its fictitious
We are fortuitous
To make it through at times

Honesty
Reminds us
Of how we show and tell
And its torturous
Tumultuous
Binds us under its spell

And just like a bell
It jars us
Disciplines us right
Because try as we might
Our only fight
Is hindsight
That's right
All we get is hindsight
It's not right
But it's how we learn
Because honesty and loyalty
Only gets us burned

So as we turn
It becomes our blindside
We learn to ignore
And on it goes on

This world we create
We're regardless
We are relentless
Our pursuit of happiness
Remorseless
So release the stress
Put to the test

The desire to achieve
Soulfulness
The dream
Less the mess
No need to impress
Happiness
The extreme

But the reality
Is meaningless
Mostly nothingness
Emptiness
Loneliness
It cuts deep inside

So in our pursuit
In this desperate race
We step on others
Just to save face
We try to deny it
With rigor and valor
But truth be told
We know our true colors
What we will do
What we will hide
How desperate we are
To jump from this ride

Complex souls
We each all are
Our morals and ethics
So so afar
We try to hide it
We try to agree
But we all know that
We all can't see

So somewhere out there
Something must be
Must have a plan
For all and me

This life
Our affliction
This addiction
It holds us
We live for each day
No matter what
We might say
We still get up
Ready to play

This game
And we do
Each and every one of you
It's our reason
Distinction
It sets us all apart

No rhyme
And no reason
We are who we are
We humans are a legion
An army
Of war
Drowning in our sorrows
Living in the burrows
Sinking
And sinning
But living for tomorrow

THE PEOPLE

The people
The only people in my life
Let's talk about them
Because we are connected
Respected
Alone in our perspectives
Protected
Expect it
They are the only ones I can trust
With my love
With my glory
My one true story
Remove it
Replace it
If only you could taste it
The feelings of this ride
Everything aside
You feel it
You embrace it
I don't even have to try

And when you cry
And when you fall
I will be there for us
And when you trust
Or when you fall
Or when you lose
Or make the wrong call
I will be there
For you and us
In love I trust
And love stands with all
Because we stand united
Truly connected
You know what I mean
You know what you dream
The one true partner
In how you choose to believe

Is the one that's the one
In how you choose to perceive
Your Brother or your Sister
Father or Mother
Uncle or Auntie
Cousin or not
It's the one you joke with
Laugh with and stand with
Giggle or snuggle
Compare all the muscle
The one you roll with
The one you come home to

Either way
You are there to stay
You breathe my words
Whichever way they turn
You call for me
Stay with me
Blow my heart and mind
Considering the words
The joys and the worst
Comparing all of these things
You always win
You watch over me
Hold me
Whisper me a story
Wake up with every morning
Accompany my journey
Through every path of day

Holding my hand
Wandering through this land
Aspiring to be
The one true me
Bringing out the best
And all of the rest

Thinking of restoring
Our innocent view of the world
Basing my words
On one whole verse
I can begin to depicter you
Watching picture slides
Drawn in pencil
Flicking over
In slow motion
I see doves
Fluttering in a motionless sky
As my eyes move to the bottom
Of the slide show in motion

And I see a mountain
With two ants at the top
Standing upright
Looking above
The sky is blue
The sun shining in the distance
Rays enveloping the scene
Almost pointing they are
At what they are seeing
Almost so close
That they are one being
And they are looking to the doves
Doing the same thing
Flying in the sunrise
Almost so close they are one being
And now I can see it
I can't help but just think
What if we are doing
The exact same thing

Connected
Expected
Two people as one
Of all the thoughts
And all the desires
You are the one

That feels and aspires
You match me at ground level
You reach me at a higher level
You exceed even my wildest
Of ever-growing dreams

So I say to you now
What I say to you always
I will always be here
To crush all of your fears
Never be gone
From my position right here
This is me
And you are you
Never will be through
Just me and you
Sometimes in life
Something just comes along
Parks itself and says
This is where I belong
In our lives
Here to stay
And there are words to say
And slides to play
So wander away
To that place in your heart
And play your slides
Right from the start

And at the end
Believe in yourself
For when you are ready
It will find you itself
And you will be scared
And you will be wary

But never forget
The unspoken words
The feelings and reasons
Dreams and allusions
That you are here and so am I
Standing as one
Beneath the sky
Whisper no words
Only show connections
Show only the draw
The mystery and reason
Why we are still together
Through all of the seasons

QUESTIONS

I see
Again
It's me
With a pen
Just saying
Writing
Explaining
All the things I'm thinking
Wondering
Believing
Wanting
Seeing
It's just me
You will see
I live like this
In a good way
And if I may
I am going to stay
And continue what I am doing
Because this is what I do
I read
I write
Draw from my might
Whisper in the night
Sleeping tight
Waking right
Try as I might
As much as I like
To be happy
Trigger happy
Live my life in happiness
Live our life in the wilderness
No her name is not our
But her is a she
And she is we
To her I will always refer
To me
And to me and her

As I try to write this thing
This thing that I am lost in
This stream of words
I've lost the verse
Don't know what I'm writing
Or even what I'm thinking
What is it
This
That
Who
You
What
Where
When
Is that allowed
Mmmm what you thinking
Yea I hear what you're saying
And what is that
About the tv playing
An advert about something
I forget what it was about
I just know I got lost
In what I was thinking
Right back at that time
I was thinking about her
That she was unhappy
About something I did
Not that I will tell you
What it is
I refer to it only
As I made a mistake
And I had made her cry
And I had made a mess
Something so simple
So small and silly
Really
Why
What's wrong with my kind
Why don't we get it
Seriously

Why
Anyway who knows
Why we have to come to blows
Verbal blow mind
I mean come on
Really
But still they are battles
And one ends in victory
So hollow and empty
And the other one struggles
Comes out of it later
When things are said and done
And you forget who had won
Just lasting effects
And scars on the heart
Empty threats
That are full of remorse
There will always be
Rows we say
Just never let them
Out run a day
Never sleep
Until our lips meet
So okay
Thought about it
And I still feel bad
So I'm going to
Raise my hand
And slap it clean
Across my face
Silly boy
Stupid man
Grow a pair
She is your biggest fan
And you are hers
So get over your fears
Heal the scars
And rise again
I have no idea
Why I thought of this

I mean come on
What is this
Am I being sad
Thoughtful
Or mad
I don't know
Why I am saying this
Doing this
Even reading it
All I know
Is what I know
Funny you know
How things go
Questions
Emotions
Provocations
Explanations
Imaginations
Wild
Running
Like major things
Conditions
Reality
Boom
Back
Just like that
Let's say
Let's hit the hay
Got to make way
Away
Today
Just say
Let's do it
Let's go
Let's question
Fix and repair
Lay it all bare
But have
Hold
And forever be there

WAKE UP

Here we go
My darkest days
Trapped in a maze
A downward spiral
Lost all my senses
My heart went viral
Open and exposed
While every door closed
People taking shots
All I had was lost
My exposure was frightening
The drama ever heightening
I had had enough
The endless potluck
Taking my chances
Not getting very far
Behind the wheel of my car
Driving away
Lost in my mind
Ignore that right turn
Keep going in a straight line
Run the road
Until the fuel runs out
Am I getting out
Free from the maze
Have I overcome
This darkest phase

Gone with the craze
Followed the leaders
Listened to society
The wanters and believers
The ones that hope
The ones that dream
And for all who stay real
This is my dream
But first I had to move on

Kick on and face up
This is enough
The dark days are over
I'm taking control
Dusting myself down
Turning it all around
Bursting through the doors
Avoiding the traps
I want to get better
Not paper over the cracks

See self-motivation
Is the hardest to find
The biggest challenge
Of your overworked mind
We listen to society
And let people hurt us
We live in fear
Of what non-compliance can do to us
Pay the bills
Pay that fine
Work for your taxes
That money is now mine
Freedom of speech
But our voices are never heard
Treated like cattle
Just one great herd
We spend most of our time
Working and dreaming
It is so hard
To never stop believing

When life takes its toll
And you break through the bandwidth
You can go crazy
Depressed or lonely
Stick a label on it
Insane or mad
Just make sure you realize
That you have been had

Because that is not it
It's grinding you down
It's making you frown
But there is a new show in town
Be it your lover
Or another
You will get your chance
To enjoy another
Another drink or another laugh
And you can put behind you
Any troubles from your past
Just think about it
Caress it
Mould it and shape it
Etch it to your canvass
And create your masterpiece

I alluded to my pain
The whirlwind I span in
Could never take a breath
Kept failing the tests
Drowned in my sorrows
Lived off what I borrowed
Lost my pride
My esteem and soul

Lost sight of my might
The truth somewhere inside
But when I uncovered it
Enlightenment prevailed
I discovered my ability
To succeed when I fail
To learn from my mistakes
To give when I take
To consider
Deliver
And a whole lot more

I learnt from the dark days
What life meant to me
I had my moment
When I was plucked from obscurity
And whether you find it
Whatever it may be
Maybe just maybe
You heard it from me
Or if not
You heard it from you
Just never forget
Always let it ring true

THE SYSTEM

The system
Existing
Spinning round and round
Just feeding
Just owning
The people on the ground
Crumbs from the table
The retail
The detail
The stress
What a mess
Career
Choice
This is the last stand
The last fight
Last rites
So tight
In spite
It might
Become right
To my delight
I do it
All despite
The challenges I face
The sacrifices I make
It's all give and take
But imbalanced
Unfair
Leaves me in despair
The rewards
Are great
Worth everything, I make
Opportunity
Cost
The benefit
Of what I've lost
And stood to gain
And won in vain

I tolerate the mistakes
Corrected will I make
The stumble
The fall
Because through it all
I've dropped the ball
But picked it up
Strutted my stuff
It's never enough
But I know
I'm breathing
Still going
All is good
In the hood
I'm on it
I got it
I have it
I chase it
And I'm here
And your here
We are here
Together
Forever
Loves letter
Gets better
We get married
Have kids
Live it for what it is
And cherish it
Remember it
For all that it is
And will become
Us as one
Work
Life
Balance
Just juggling it is
Spinning the plates
Finding the middle
The even ground

The equilibrium
The composer
The artist
Capturing a still of time
Making the moment come alive
Whispering the reason
In your ear
And you hear
What's near
In the future
The hope
Once in the distance
Drifting towards the present
And we are inspired
And we strive to win
We go again
And we want it
Dream it
Relive it
Experience it
Rejoice in it
And stay true to the words
For granted
So we respect
Reflect
And wonder at the vision
But stay true
When you're feeling blue
Perk up
That's enough
Fortune is on its way
The system
Its tainted
We all know it's true
But we must stay strong
If we are to live long
So for right or wrong
Accept it is done

The system is ours
We cannot run
All we can do
Is live life true
Take it and go with it
Because the system is you

MONEY

It's funny
Money
It drives us
Reminds us
Finds us
It's always
Part of the plan

You had it
I had it
We both had something
You got it
You lost it
I paid the gamble and lost

I hoped and dreamed
And when it seemed
Like all was won
And negative lost
It finds a way
To pull you back taught

Try as I might
I will always fight
But this damn war
Never draws near
I shout at a distance
Scream at a mile
Climbing the waterfall
And forever falling down

It comes
It goes
Wind rain or snow
I know
It is gone
To one day come back
It talks to me in riddles

Always playing second fiddle
Never knowing
Who will have
The last laugh
What way will it go
Who knows where to next
I've been naive
I've been brave
Only now do I know
How to behave

I've learnt
From my mistakes
Given way more
Than I could ever take
And for heaven's sake
Upon reflection
I remember my dreams
My wants
And desires
For a win
Of some kind
A fix
A trick
That is what it is
The gloves coming off
Spending what I want
Blurring the lines
Nothing is enough
Not tough
Not exposed
Always enough
Money is never closed

It dictates us
Estimates us
Wrecks us
Warns us
Warms us
Comforts us

Haunts us
Exposes us
Draws us all in
To the game
It's paying
It's playing
To win
Toying
Like puppets on a string
Motionless
Homeless
Controlled
On hold

It's a debate
The two
Money and life
A negotiation
A motion
A whisper or a whim
It tempts me
Leads me
Redemption
Exemption
Relentless
Expect it
To drag you to the depths
The bottom
The well
Cylindrical walls
Damp
Dank
Nowhere left to fall
At the bottom
A piece of wasteland
Wet
Miserable
Unbelievable
Unthinkable
Unimaginable strife

I struggle
To ascertain
To explain where I've been
It was hard
To live
Without the last laugh
Not a dime
Was mine
No cash
To splash
Just water
Running
Straining
Draining
Through my sieve of a hand

When I stand
There is nowhere to go
No end
No gaps
Cracks
Whatever
Just walls
And darkness
And a pinprick of light
Up high
In the sky
The heavens
Good heavens
How far down am I
What do I try
Hope is lost
Can I find
Rewind
Back through time

I may find
The piece that gets me out
So I can shout
Celebrate

The end of the mess I made
So I can soar
Once more
Walking with the gods
And there it is
Doing it again
Going there
To that place
The mindset
I'm conditioned with
Imagining what life is like
Invading my mind
With no respite
Ignoring reality
With devastating consequences
Because the truth is this
It does not currently exist
I'm scared
I'm there
Wake up to a nightmare
To get there
There are no stairs
Beyond reproach
I'm totally broke
I can't even smoke
Or eat a good meal
The end of hope
The end is nigh
The only thing to try
Is to fall to more
But guess what
I couldn't
There was nowhere left to fall

So I stood tall
Re-addressed
Assessed
And noticed
Something at the wall
A rung

A hook
A climb
For some time
But a ladder
Nevertheless
There is a chance after all
And if I make it
And I do not fall
If I try hard enough
I can start all over again

And on that journey
That perilous journey
I had temptation
I had hard calls
Making decisions
To stay within rhythm
To get to the top
Don't stop till I drop
And if I don't drop
I get to the top
Climb out of the abyss
And start to exist
To mean something
Know something
Be somebody
Make life about me
Wander about
With lessons learnt
Live my life
With money I've earnt

That I reflect
Respect
Select
Deflect
Reject
What do you expect
I elect
Control

To have and to hold
Feeding the desires
Reigning in
Hook and loop
Cautious approach
Never will I breach
The line
In the sand
Of money I don't have
I am not being had
Or bad
Or naughty
Just me
And my finances
Respecting the consequences
Churning through numbers
Crunchers
Munchers
Shedding the incompetence
It's all in the evidence
Smartening up

And if I get stuck
I instruct
Consciences
Sensibleness
Is that a word
Instead
Responsible then
And then
It is me
With a pen
And rhymes
And words
Between the lines
This time
Chapter six
It's mine
It's yours
It's ours

Our message
Our mantra
Our karma
Forever
And ever

Money
It's funny
How we all live our lives
In love with our minds
And losing it
Regaining it
Repositioning it
Nervous disposition
Dangerous comparisons
Liaisons
Occasions
Elevations
And tunes
And times
Memories
Enemies
Voices
Choices
Wrong ones
Right ones
Must have ones
Never had ones
Always had ones
Always wanted ones
Fun ones
Only ones
Just the one
The only one

The last gasp
The farce
The task
The thing
That I tell you

Always will it own you
The thing I can tell me
Is between me and me
So now
The end
Of this chapter
A feel-good factor
Happy ending
I got my dream
And it will never run
Out of steam
Close my eyes
And all I see
Is my prize
My worth
My savior
My love
My one

And guess what it cost me
Not a single one
Not even half of one
Not one penny
Not one thing
Just a chance
A stroke of fortune
A pinprick of light
The end in sight
And what a thing
Irony is
Because the end in sight
Was just the beginning
I'm singing
Exploding
Running out of the blocks
Beating the clocks
Eating
Sleeping
Living
Relieving

Just stop
I stop now
This was supposed to be about money
But I say it again
Again mention irony
Because isn't it funny
Love doesn't cost anything
Not one thing
Don't you worry
Not a thing
Not even money

VOICES

When I write
It looks right
Sounds right
Feels right
The voices in my head
I'm telling you instead
Piecing the pictures
Together
I'm with you
Feeling it
Reading it
Writing it I am

Envisioning the visions
Speaking the rhythms
The rhymes
The times
I'm telling you I'm fine
It's the voices
They are flowing
Fleeting
Fluttering
My train of thought
Chugging
Churning
Translating on the page

Call me insane
But that's how it goes
Laying out on paper
When I meet my maker
That's what I will say
I had no part to play
In all the words spoken
Whoever has awoken
Speaks through me
Taking over my mind
As I am so kind

I just let it happen
I am but a vessel
For whatever this is
Inspiration
Levitation
Out of my mind
Sub conscious
Religious
Who knows what you will find

But what I know
Is not what I write
I read it after
The same as you
Where did it come from
What is it about
How did all of this
Ever come about
I don't know
How it happens
I see something out there
And then it all starts

A sentence
An explosion
Then the bells ring
My mind starts to sing
My finger stings
Tingles
Sparkles
Heralds the arrival
Of the written word
And now I need a platform
A pad
A pen
A phone
An empty home
An environment of peace
Then it comes
All out in one

I finish it
I read it
I speak it
I record it
And then there it is
A masterpiece
On the precipice
Of maybe something great

So what's it all for
This journey
This course
Who knows
What do I know
I'm just the vessel of course
It comes to me
Some how
And I give it the respect it deserves
And when it goes
I speak and show
So proud of the next verse

Desperate for
Your feedback and advice
I listen to your impression
Your notions
Expectations
Your visions
Understanding
The message between the lines
I get it
You get it
Maybe it helps some how
Maybe it is here
To help those who fear
To inspire those who need
To calm those crazy thoughts
Alleviate depression
Or have all the answers

That I do not
But I can help make you smile
Or wonder for a while
Make you laugh
Bring relief at last
Think about good things
Happy thoughts
Peaceful thoughts
Hopefully I can bring
To the journey you are in
There has to be a reason
Why this has come about
And I tell you now
I will give it what it deserves
Respect it in turn
Give it a platform
To shine on its own

Me with a pen
You again
Listening to the words
Be it chapter or verse
Poem or story
In all its glory
I hope you approve
And are in a good mood
Thanks for listening
Or reading
Or interpreting
Analyzing
Expecting
Believing
Not rejecting
You have given me a chance
And I give you my mind
Forever in your debt
I'm thanking you in kind

CHAPTER SEVEN

THE END

The final steps on this journey were due to be taken. The last pieces in my tale of 'love and heartbreak' needed to be written. The oscillation from 'darkness to light' and then again from 'light to darkness' taught me that life is cyclical indeed and if I accepted this, I could become energized from this cycle. I was now ready to embrace the change that was waiting for me. I had gone through six stages that guided my writing and I was now ready for the seventh. The darkness turned to fog, the fog to haze, the haze to shadows. What was once a mere spot of light was now enveloping the scene, burning away all before it. As the shadows burned, the final words in the final chapter of this book emerged. My dreams, thoughts, hopes and fears. My memories, my aches and my tears – all captured in this collection. My heart has spoken, my mind has spoken, my soul has spoken.

These four poems express my journey into *emergence*:

1. DREAM
2. WE WERE IN LOVE
3. IMAGINE
4. WHAT REMAINS

DREAM

What is the point
In searching for love
For I have already found it
And lost it the same

My time had come
But now is past
Now I cannot see
For it is gone too fast

All I can feel
Is absolute emptiness
There is no hope
There is no end to this

All that I have
Is a future alone
Because I've already had
A girl on the throne

Having met the one
More than once
Now they are gone
All that is done

I grew up dreaming
Of my dream girl
But that dream has now gone
As my life unfolds

I've unraveled my soul
And let them all in
But now I am left
With only emptiness within

For my heart is scarred
And now slightly black
I can never hope
To ever go back

I've lived a dream
More than once
But the damage is done
It's cold in my core

Fool me once
Fool me twice
I tried it a third time
And it wasn't so nice

I invested everything
Gave it my all
All for a moment
Just waiting to fall

My dream is over
It has all collapsed
I can't do it again
I think that's a fact

And it is so sad
Because I had so much to give
But the motivation has left me
Such a pain is this

The dream is gone
The reality of a nightmare
I know it is harsh
I know it isn't fair

Yet all I can do now
Is tape over the cracks
And when that is done
I will turn my back

Turn it I must
Because I can't do this again
I can't fake the dream
My love can't extend

I can't reach out
For I have nothing left
So all I can do
Is make the best

I will live this life
Holding memories dear
But to make new ones
I will only have fear

I wish I could dream
But that dream is dead
I now stay alone
It fills me with dread

Maybe I have been tested
Given experience
So that I can give my everything
When the one comes along

Maybe I should stop searching
Or never should have
That hindsight is obvious
It just ends up bad

But one thing is for sure
I must not regret
The dream was amazing
Lest I forget
I thank all those
Who gave me a chance

I do wish it worked
I wish I can glance
Back to the past
And put things right

But I know I can't do that
So I shall no longer fight
Is this what my next dream will be
For if it is about love
It will be without me

WE WERE IN LOVE

We held hands
Took to the stands
A two-person band
We were in love

We hugged
Kissed
We were living in bliss
Cuddled and caressed
We were in love

We toured the country
Seeing new sights
We travelled beyond
Climbing new heights

We scoured the globe
On new adventures
Drank and laughed
With careless whispers
Chitted and chatted
Swaying in the light
We could go crazy
We could go all night

We were a force
You and me
A force to be reckoned with
We were in love

We entertained and dined
With the finest wine
Not that I drank it
Not that I'd mind

We ate the finest
We were so keen
Too many places
Living the dream

Looked up to the stars
Stood by the sea
Shared our whole lives away
We were in love

We drove everywhere
We walked everywhere
Toured mountains
Watched eagles
Mingled with locals
We felt so humbled

A thousand photos
Even some videos
Play it on the stereo
We were in love

We swam at resorts
Chuffed champagne
We knew we were changing
Changing the game

We did hotels
Circled wells
Visited castles
Played kiss and tell
Board games
Puzzles
Films and cinema
All you could think of
We were in love

The romance was hot
The music was loud
Anything was possible
It could be found

We were invincible
We fit like a glove
Showered in glory
We were in love

We were soul mates
Destined for greatness
We were together
With life so limitless
But just like the rain
The end is inevitable
We were exposed to it
Just as fallible
Will always be truth
That we were the one
Despite the ending
We were in love

IMAGINE

I saw someone today
A love from the past
A friend in the present
For sure in the future
A beautiful soul
Who touches my heart
We are set apart
But our connection is vast
Built to last
Indeed it will
It's not a cheap thrill
It's the real deal

We have a bond
So strong and true
What binds us
I haven't a clue
I just know it is there
Burning inside
So I begin to twist it
Turn to rewind

Play it all back
To the moment we were
Imagine what
If you could have been her
The one
And only
The elusive one
The one I've dreamed for
The one true love
Imagine it had happened
All so differently
Imagine if we had been
We had been you and me

And as I ponder
On all I would take back
I imagine
The future
If it got took back
The relationships I have had
All the hurt I've felt there

But all the experiences
I've lived to endure
So much happiness
So much sadness
So much life I'd miss
My mind would not be the same
Yes of course the dream
It would all be worth it
But I must conclude
I'm better off for it

For all of the loves
I've felt ever since
All of the beauty
The banter and bliss
When it all comes down to it
I lost them like this
Each one has come
And gone like this

What can I say
It always goes wrong
But it's nice to reminisce
To wonder once was
To ponder and embrace
With no love lost
Everyone
Every moment
Held in my heart
In every moment

Imagine
Rewind
What could have been

Think
What if
It always had been

But then
Your mind
Is in overdrive
Because how can you contemplate
Leaving all behind

You can't
Because you won't
Because it's made you who you are
It's nice to imagine
Reach out so far

But now it's time
To build the future
Let go of our pasts
And be something better

WHAT REMAINS

So what remains
After it's all gone
Memories faded
An empty throne

A desolate wasteland
I must now assess
The remains of the past
Remains of distress

How has it left me
What has it done
What will I make of it
What will I become

So on reflection
I made myself step up
Looked to stay positive
Made myself tough

In all fairness
It has kind of worked
If I'm perfectly honest
I'm making it work

I get up
Each and every day
Making the most
In every way
Sad but it's true
It just is the case
It's empty happiness
Just to keep face

As it might sound tragic
I really don't mind
To tell you the truth
I just love being kind

I like to help
I want to give
In any way
To help how to live

So despite the fact
I have no goals
I know every day
They will always come

Challenges I face
I tackle head on
I control the impression
That I'm feeling strong

I do these things
I live this lie
When it feels like reality
Is I'm dying inside

It's not dramatic
Just my flame is burnt out
I have no fear
I have no doubt

My path is hazy
As I stumble on forward
It doesn't faze me
Each day as it comes

So overall
I have a smile on my face
Try to be polite
Live it with grace

Take it easy
Let time do its thing
Keep telling myself that
Making the bell ring

Aimless
Directionless
Frictionless
Motionless
It hurts if I try

So I go with the flow
Because it's all that remains
An empty canvas
An open plain

Thirty odd years
And life has thrown everything
Heaven and earth
Have shifted beneath my feet

Knocks and punches
Kicks and screams
Good and the bad
Everything in-between

It's taken my heart
It's ground down my soul
Grinded my mind
And made me fold

It's twisted me
Wrapped me
Bent me up inside
Yet somehow it's fulfilled me
And made me feel alive

This life
Its fate
The feelings it makes
Worth all the sacrifice
It's all at stake

Every day
In every way
Still got to stay sharp
To live another day

In all I can write
And all I can say
It is what remains
On this present day

It's all I know
And all I see
It's what remains
What's left of me

I might seem damaged
But I'm honestly not
This was the time
To hit that spot

The final nail
The box of all boxes
An end of an era
One for the ages

Its time is up
Time to move on
To walk from the past
And into the future

This one is closed
The moment now past
I must now build
A brand-new path

For now, is the path
To aftermath
To shape what happens
What will become

Whatever happens
After all that's been
I will embrace the moments
Live it so keen

Every corner
All the turns
I am a free soul
And continue to learn

I've discovered myself
Throughout all these pages
Laid it all bare
Emptied the cages

You have but my mind
You've read it all
A journey through
Straight through my soul

I gave you my hand
You gave me your heart
Thank you for reading
For giving a chance

It has been a journey
And honestly a pleasure
My gratitude fair reader
Will live on forever

To Be Continued...

Instagram @leon.gregori213
Facebook @leon.gregori213
www.allpoetry.com/Leon_Gregori

Made in the USA
Monee, IL
12 April 2020

25558896R10164